IRAN
THE GREEN MOVEMENT

By: Slater Bakhtavar

THE
STRUGGLE
CONTINUES

THE
GREEN
MOVEMENT

THE STRUGGLE CONTINUES

Җ

SLATER BAKHTAVAR

ISBN 978-0-578-03325-9 (softcover)

ISBN 978-0-578-03552-9 (hardcover)

Published in the United States by

Parsa Enterprises, LLC

Irving, Texas 75063

Manufactured in the United States of America

10 9 8 7 6 5 4 3 2 1

Artwork design by Amin Abedi

Photography by Hamed Saber

Author's Biography

Slater Bakhtavar, an Iran native, is a published journalist, policy analyst, and practicing attorney. His interest in politics has enabled him to contribute his knowledge to several journals, magazines, and nationally syndicated talk shows. Additionally, Slater is actively involved in analyzing foreign policy for various organizations.

Slater has earned a bachelor's degree in political science from Kennesaw State University, a Juris Doctorate from South Texas College of Law, and a LL.M in International Law from Loyola Law School. In addition, Slater Bakhtavar received a certificate in alternative dispute resolution from the University of Georgia Law Center.

Currently, Slater resides in Dallas, Texas, where he is engaged in the practice of law at his own law office. Outside of his law practice, Slater can be found devoting his time to The Republican Youth of America organization, where he sits as the founding president. To add to his myriad list of activities and accomplishments, Slater has decided to pursue a master of business administration degree from West Texas A&M. Even with his busy schedule and various activities that he participates in, Slater Bakhtavar spends his spare time at the gym and playing sports.

Dedicated to my brother, my parents, my family, close friends, and the Iranian people.

—Slater Bakhtavar

TABLE OF CONTENTS

I N T R O D U C T I O N		EPITOME OF CHANGE
C H A P T E R 1	١	IRAN'S STRUCTURE OF GOVERNMENT
C H A P T E R 2	٢	1999 STUDENT UPRISINGS
C H A P T E R 3	٣	DAWN OF THE UPRISINGS
C H A P T E R 4	٤	DAYS THAT FOLLOWED
C H A P T E R 5	٥	THE FACE OF THE 1999 STUDENT UPRISINGS
C H A P T E R 6	٦	2000 PRESIDENTIAL ELECTIONS
C H A P T E R 7	٧	A PRELUDE TO THE "GREEN MOVEMENT"
C H A P T E R 8	٨	AHMADINEJAD'S UNSUCCESSFUL TERM
C H A P T E R 9	٩	LEAD UP TO THE 2009 ELECTIONS
C H A P T E R 10	١٠	JUNE 12, 2009: ELECTION DAY
C H A P T E R 11	١١	DEMONSTRATIONS IN THE STREETS
C H A P T E R 12	١٢	UNREST CONTINUES
C H A P T E R 13	١٣	KHAMENEI BREAKS SILENCE
C H A P T E R 14	١٤	DEATH OF NEDA
C H A P T E R 15	١٥	REPRESSION GROWS
C H A P T E R 16	١٦	OFFICIALS BLAME THE WEST
C H A P T E R 17	١٧	INTERNAL DIVISIONS MOUNT
C H A P T E R 18	١٨	BASIJ ON THE OFFENSIVE
C H A P T E R 19	١٩	ANNIVERSARY OF THE 1999 UPRISINGS
C H A P T E R 20	٢٠	CALM BEFORE THE STORM

CHAPTER 21   ٢١   FIRST DEPUTY RESIGNATION

CHAPTER 22   ٢٢   AHMADINEJAD'S INAUGURATION

CHAPTER 23   ٢٣   SHOWDOWN FOR THE AYATOLLAHS

CHAPTER 24   ٢۴   THE WORLD TURNS GREEN

CHAPTER 25   ٢۵   THE MOVEMENT'S PLACE IN HISTORY

CHAPTER 26   ٢۶   THE TECHNOLOGICAL REVOLUTION

CHAPTER 27   ٢٧   WHERE THE MOVEMENT IS HEADED

CONCLUSION   THE WORLD AWAITS A DEMOCRATIC IRAN

EPITOME OF CHANGE

In the past months, Iran has experienced the epitome of what one would consider to be a raging political war ignited by the allegedly fraudulent "democratic" presidential election that was held on June 12, 2009. In hopes to gain international attention, many Iranian citizens have challenged Iran's Clerical Regime (the Islamic Republic) by continuous rebellion through demonstrations, protests, and outright defiance directed at the Iranian government. In reaction to this defiance, the hard-line Iranian leaders have made efforts to stop all noncompliant behavior by brutal, coercive force.

As this book takes shape through an in-depth discussion of the postelection events of the 2009 presidential election, it is important to note that it follows a story that is not yet complete. In other words, this is a story without an ending. I have always found it difficult to write a book that lacks an ending—the place where ideas can be "wrapped up" and conclusions can be stated. It is obvious, in support of the Iranian people, that many people hope this story never has an ending—but rather that the "Green Movement" continues on and achieves democratic change in the lives of the Iranian people and the country of Iran.

Before we can understand the potential implications and ramifications of the Iranian people's current struggle for power, it is crucial to know the history from which these events have evolved. It is a history as unique and ever-changing as the Iranian culture itself. The people of Iran are not the same in regards to beliefs and ideologies as the citizens of the 1980s and 1990s; and yet, these citizens are far different than those that lived in Iran before the Shah was overthrown in 1979. All generations of Iranian people have displayed their nationalism, pride, and fight for freedom in diverse and distinct ways; however, their objective has been more or less the same.

It's important to remember that even as you read this book, a struggle is still taking place in Iran. As long as the structure of government—what some call a falsified "democracy"—still stands, Iranian people will always be subjected to abuse and manipulation of their own government's particular agenda. This is not a fictitious story, but rather an eye-opening report of the events that are occurring behind the curtain that the Islamic Republic has blanketed their country with. As you will read, seeing what happens behind this curtain has not been easy for those outside of Iran, but because of the desperation of the Iranian people, we have been able to keep up with the news coming from the front lines.

Since the establishment of the Islamic Republic when the Shah was overthrown in 1979, many Middle Eastern researchers have suggested that Iran has experienced what they call a "thermidor." In his article, "Thermidor in the Islamic Republic of Iran: The Rise of Muhammad Khatami," Wells defines a thermidor as "the closing phase of a revolution wherein hard-line revolutionaries are increasingly challenged by reformists. It is usually a product of, and/or accompanied by, a popular backlash to revolutionary policies."[1] Although the particular thermidor Wells is referring to in his article is the one at the end of the Rafsanjani presidency, it is obvious that Iran is currently experiencing a new one.

One question we must consider is "What causes this Thermodorian theory to exist?" Scholars have come to various detailed conclusions in an attempt to answer this question, but there is one component that is common in all of their theories: A country experiencing a thermidor is often successful because of the fact that all types of reform groups, even though they might not agree with the ideas of the other, will band together just because they despise the government much more.[1] This idea is largely applicable to the current "Green Movement" in Iran because of the fact that the majority of the citizens, regardless of their beliefs, have come to the point that *anything* would be better than the current government and their hard-line practices.

CHAPTER 1

IRAN'S STRUCTURE OF GOVERNMENT

T he hierarchy of power in Iran is distinct in that it is the only country that operates a system of government that has so many different groups that attempt to balance the power distribution. Iran has not been run with this particular structure of government forever, but rather, it was only recently implemented, in relative terms. In 1979, Iran was still considered to be a monarchy when it was violently brought down by the citizens of Iran. It was only then that the Islamic Republic, what the Iranian government is considered to be today, was established.

Sitting at the top of the power structure is the supreme ruler, Ayatollah Ali Khamenei. The supreme ruler is not an elected position, but rather a position that is selected by the Assembly of Experts. This man is the head of all religious and political decisions made within the country. Underneath him are five separate divisions of differentiated powers. The supreme leader has an overwhelming influence over all of these factions of government. He is, by far, the most powerful man in Iran, and has always influenced the government leaders below him to embrace his hard-line practices and beliefs.

The current supreme leader of Iran is the semi-infamous, at least in the eyes of the Iranian citizens, Ayatollah Ali Khamenei. Khamenei has been Iran's supreme leader since the death of Ayatollah Ruhollah Khomeini, the previous supreme leader, in 1989. Khomeini was the first man to fill the supreme leader position after the monarchy was overthrown in 1979. Khamenei, the current supreme leader of Iran, is only Iran's second person to hold this most prominent position. It is important to note that the Assembly of Experts, which will soon be discussed, "theoretically" holds the power to remove the supreme leader, but this right has yet to be exercised—and likely never will.

We have arrived at the point in this system of government where it is not completely clear who is the next in importance in regards to the possession of power. Several positions of power underneath the supreme leader, like the president, for example, are arranged in a way that emanates false impressions of power. In all reality, the falsified power that the people of these positions hold is limited by opposing positions of power.

There are a total of six different self-contained entities that hold power pertaining to the inherent responsibilities of each group. These centers of power are commonly ranked, according to importance, in the following order (beginning with the most important): (1) the supreme leader, (2) the Revolutionary Guard, (3) the Guardian Council, (4) the president, (5) the parliament (i.e., Majlis), and (6) the National Security Council. These six powers regulate other political and religious organizations, like the Expediency Council, Basij militia, VEVAK, Quds Forces, and Loyalist groups.

Each of the political and/or social groups mentioned above are quite complex within their particular faction when it comes to who they answer to, control, and appoint. The Islamic Revolutionary Guard Corps is a branch of the military founded after 1979. It is considered to be the official force that regulates the country through armed coercion and operates separately from Iran's military. The commander in chief of the Revolutionary Guard, which makes this faction a channel for the funneling of his ultimate agenda, is the supreme leader. On the flip side of the coin, the Revolutionary Guard controls the Qud forces, which is a military group that equips, finances, organizes, and trains foreign Islamic revolutionary movements, and the now-infamous Basij militia, the group responsible for using extreme force to stifle the demonstrations and protests of the Iranian citizens.

Below the preeminent Islamic Revolutionary Guard Corps, in terms of importance, is the Guardian Council. It is a group that possesses great control in its efforts to stifle all endeavors that indicate in any way the smallest hint of reform and liberalization of the people. The Guardian Council is comprised of 12 authorities, six dominating hard-line clerics which then elect six less-influential jurists. It is charged with interpreting the Iranian Constitution, supervising elections of, and approving candidates to, the Assembly of Experts, the president, and parliament (Majlis). It is this group of men who have historically stomped liberal reform from rising up out of the general population and have substantially increased the power of the Islamic Revolutionary Guard Corps.

The Guardian Council has the means to prevent these common attempts at reform because they possess the privileges of: (1) controlling the execution all formal elections, (2) determining if a person is "qualified" to become a candidate of formal elections, and (3) the right to reject any proposed legislation of parliament. Unlike the

Assembly of Experts, the Guardian Council consistently exercises its power. The clerics of the Guardian Council are appointed by the supreme leader, illustrating once again, how the supreme leader has the dangerous ability to directly control the political makeup of the government he presides over. Due to the influence of this group, the Islamic Revolutionary Guards now control the majority of Iran's oil resources and have gained considerable political influence since the presidency of Mahmoud Ahmadinejad.

Ranking fourth in supremacy is the semi-democratically elected president of Iran. The previous presidents of Iran have always seemed to be a counteracting mechanism to balance the ideologies and practices of the supreme leader. With this being said, the counteracting ideas the president displays must be done in a way that doesn't blatantly undermine the other factions of government because the supreme leader oversees the president and has the ability to demote him. The president's responsibilities include maintaining close relations with the Revolutionary Guards, overseeing the Basij militants, and sitting as the chairman of the National Security Council.

The Iranian Parliament, also known as the Majlis, is the national legislative body of Iran. The Majlis currently has 290 representatives. All Majlis candidates and all legislation from the assembly must be approved by the Guardian Council. Candidates must pledge in writing that they are committed, in theory and in practice, to the Iranian Constitution.

The National Security Council is an assembly of members that is responsible for dealing with foreign policy issues, including courses of action, and acts as an advisor for all nuclear issues. This council doesn't preside over any other government faction and is led solely by the elected president.

1999 STUDENT UPRISINGS

"Everyone has the right to freedom of opinion and expression; this right includes freedom to hold opinions without interference, and to seek, receive and impart information ideas through any media and regardless of frontiers."

—Article 19 from the Universal Declaration
of Human Rights

One of the more surprising demographic facts about Iran is that 70 percent of the population is under 30 years of age. This simple statistic has molded Iran into an increasingly more modern society with a thriving and unpredictable "student population." This population that is often referred to as "Iranian youth" has been strongly linked to the generation of reformist ideas surfacing in Iran. Most of these reformist ideals are formed and passed through dialogue within the university setting. Tehran University, along with 22 additional universities throughout Iran, appeared to be the launching pad for radical ideas, reform movements, and the ongoing fight for basic human and civil rights for the Iranian people in the late 1990s.

Iran, in late 1999, was a far cry from the Iran ruled by the Shah in respect to culture and the atmosphere of the city. In Tehran, Esfahan, Shiraz, Tabriz, and many other cities, the yellow brick seminaries and mud-brick homes had been replaced with modern city scenes, complete with high-rise housing and corporate business towers. The streets had been paved, and traffic lights installed. Countless sources claim that the "youth population" of the 1990s had radically changed in their appearance, attitude, and beliefs, in comparison to their parents. It was obvious that the now-dated "pop-culture" trends of the West had hit this generation with full force and was embraced with open arms.

This youth population had no connection with the ultra-fundamentalist beliefs that the Islamic Republic had implemented, especially related to the restrictions on free speech. The attempted suppression of freedom of press and speech with Iran has also been a battle, which is obviously still being fought, that has lasted for over 30 years.

Let's take a look back at a couple of historical events that have contributed to the extreme frustration of the Iranian people in regards to their right to freedom of speech:

In September of 1980, the *Spokane Daily Chronicle*, a major U.S. newspaper, ran an article "Iranian Student Believes Communist Are Next to Rule in Iran." Throughout the article, the student complains about the lives of Iranian citizens under the rule of the supreme leader at the time, Ayatollah Khomeini. Notice that this is only one year after the establishment of the new "Islamic Republic" that was supposedly going to save the people from the Shah. The student, Hamideh Ramjerdi, comments, "The new Islamic government is hardly more objective than the late Shah's tribunals." Complaining about the harsh restrictions on freedom of press implemented by the Islamic Republic, she says, "… democracy would be the ideal government for Iran, a government where there would be freedom of speech and religion, and separation of church and state."

In 1989, Supreme Leader Khomeini showcased his strict restrictions on freedom of speech when he sentenced Salam Rushdie, author of the book, *Satanic Verses*, to death for the publication of his writings. Ayatollah Khomeini was quoted as saying, "I inform the proud Muslim people of the world that the author of the *Satanic Verses* book, which is against Islam, the Prophet, and the Koran, and all those involved in its publication who are aware of its content, are sentenced to death."

An Iranian affairs analyst who lives inside Iran explains that when Khatami, the reformist president, was elected, he tried to lift the death sentence against Salam Rushdie. This decision by Khatami sparked a huge debate between the conservatives in power with Khamenei sitting as supreme leader and the reformist public. The Iranian analyst, Sadeq Saba, offers this in his analysis of the situation: "The hard-liners are opposed to President Khatami's efforts to improve relations with the West and with the United Kingdom, in particular. They know that the West is sensitive about the fate of Mr. Rushdie, and they deliberately insist on implementing the fatwa in order to thwart Mr. Khatami's efforts." Even today, in 2009, there is still a reward for the killing of Salam Rushdie, which is set at 2.8 million dollars.

Of course, this leads us to the reason for the highly publicized student uprising of 1999, the closing of the *Salam* newspaper. Khatami was president at this time and press, media, and speech restrictions had seemed to lessen, but not by any significant measure. We will address this issue in far greater detail next.

To the Iranian people, the politically charged year of 1999 will always be remembered as one of the most significant political student rebellions since the fall of the Shah in 1979. The extreme methods of defiance used against the theocratic government represented the solid stand the student population of Iran was willing to take in hopes to end the extreme violation of their civil and human rights. The 10th anniversary of this tragic event was observed as this book was being written, and more details about it will follow.

The months that led up to July 1999 were filled with political unrest within the student population, mainly in the city of Tehran. With more reformist ideas populating the university than ever before, the students of Tehran University were convinced that the fundamentalist theories of the Islamic Republic were robbing the citizens of Iran of their most basic rights.

During this time, the theocratic government was encouraging the students of Tehran University and the youth of the general public to participate in political activities. This encouragement from the Islamic Republic came with only one stipulation:

These activities must support the ideals and theories of the Islamic Republic and in no way challenge them. This type of "encouragement," on behalf of the Islamic Republic, illustrates the way in which the fundamentalists create *illusions* of democracy but restrict it with rigid stipulations, totally violating the definition of democracy.

Constant acts of democratic manipulation by the Islamic Republic, like the one stated above, only further confirmed, in the minds of the Iranian youth, the notion that this Islamic Republic must be overthrown in order for a true democracy to exist in Iran. The student population felt that there was no possibility of acquiring a democratic government with such fundamentalists holding the reins of the leadership structure.

Only 2 years prior to the 1999 student uprisings, the politically active student population had played a large part in electing Mohammad Khatami as Iran's president. At this time, the universities within Iran were thriving with student activists and had become the hub of radical political dialogue. University students were beginning to form student organizations focused on their beliefs of what government should be. On the university campuses, students could be seen buzzing with enthusiasm for new ideals and a new life within their country.

Khatami was a supporter of these student organizations during the months that led up to the presidential election, hoping that in some way he could utilize the groups to push his own agenda. It must be noted that he did not use the students for their support, but rather, that is the group that his beliefs and visions for the future of Iran aligned with. Much credit for the success of the sudden upsurge of student-led activism has been linked to Khatami, specifically during the time of his 1997 presidential campaign. After the presidential election of 1997, Mohammad Khatami was announced as Iran's newest president. Many political analysts suggested that Khatami was responsible for establishing student-run political organizations and it was these organizations that were largely responsible for his successful election.

It wasn't long after the election of Khatami when change, politically, socially, and religiously, started to become visible in regards to human rights and the liberalization of the Iranian people. Khatami had remained true to his promises of a more democratic government; however, in the end, he failed the Iranian people. He felt the hard-line attitudes of the theocracy only bred more hard-line opposition from the student population. By allowing more open reform activities among the citizens of Iran, Khatami was showered with support and praise by the people of Iran (especially students of the universities). He strategically used the political momentum, which he gained from this support, in his endeavors to overcome the hard-line, conservative traditions of the Islamic Republic.

It quickly became obvious that the "youth population" of Iran saw Khatami as the only person that could improve their quality of life by facilitating change within the governmental structure. The enthusiasm shown by Khatami supporters led to an even more severe divide between two different groups of people, the reformists and the traditionalists. This discord led to the Clerical Regime's harsh crackdown on any reform activity. The government began to implement restrictions on free press and severely violated the basic rights of its citizens.

In his article, "From Revolution to Revelations: Khatami's Iran Struggles for Reform," Genieve Abdo states, "It is this freedom which conservatives fear the most: society's newfound courage to criticize the establishment openly; the public demand for action when intellectuals are murdered; and even the newly granted right of unmarried couples to sit in a Tehran café. All of these liberties have evolved since Khatami came to power." There is no question that this statement is true and that, indeed, it is this very freedom that the hard-liners fear.

One might begin to ask himself, what harm is there in having fearful hard-liners? The answer lies in the actions of the hard-liners, like the ones that were seen in July 1999.

As July approached, a political group known as the Iranian People's Party began to publically voice their opinion and goals of their party. In an interview with the chairman of the European branch of the Iranian People's Party, Mehran Adib claims, "We are fighting for freedom of speech, freedom of the press, and the realization of human rights in Iran. We do not want a totalitarian regime but a democratically elected representation of the people. We also advocate a separation of the state and religion."

We will see how the Iranian People's Party plays an active role in the events on July 9, 1999, in the next section.

DAWN OF THE UPRISINGS

The morning of July 9, 1999, was said by many to be a normal summer day on the campus of Tehran University. By this point in time, the students had formed many political student organizations in an attempt to gain support for their fight for basic human rights and separation of powers between church and state. There were no visible indications of major student uprisings or physical political dissidence, but there were the ordinary cases of many students protesting, in a peaceful manner, on the campus of Tehran University.

News of the approved court order, in regards to the closing of the *Salam* newspaper, didn't take long to spread throughout the student population at Tehran University. The *Salam* was a reformist newspaper that was published daily and read by many Iranians. The government claimed that *Salam* had published a letter in the paper that threatened "national oppositionists" and revealed the murders of five other oppositionists, otherwise known as reform activists. The government viewed this printing as encouraging dissidence within the population. The leaking of this information by *Salam* heightened the government's fear that this would cause an increase in student dissent. To remind the population just how hard-line the theocracy is, the *Salam* was ordered to shut down immediately.

To the students and other political activists, this was the breaking point. In their minds, this was the last time their right to freedom of speech would be violated by the Islamic Republic. The time had come for the student population, among others, to unite and create a solid stand in their recognition for human and civil rights. It is important to recognize that this generation of Iranians, almost every person under the age of 30, does not feel the least bit aligned with the ideologies or practices of the Islamic Republic. They live in a country that doesn't represent their generation in anyway whatsoever.

The organization most recognized for coordinating the first demonstration in response to the closure of the *Salam* newspaper was the Bureau of Consolidation of Unity (BCU). The BCU called for all those in support of political reform to participate in the first demonstration for human rights. Much to the BCU's surprise, they learned that students attending Tehran University had already launched a peaceful demonstration on the campus of the university.

It wasn't but a matter of minutes before the Basij militia, influenced and instructed solely by the Islamic Republic, had shown up on the Tehran University campus. By this time, the peaceful demonstration was over and the group of students had already returned to their dorm rooms. The state police came in with 200 officers strong. These militia men, dressed in street clothes, ambushed students in the dorms. After breaking in, they ran through the hallways attacking anyone in their path. There was one reported fatal shooting. Other students were shot, and many were brutally beaten. Many students were interviewed and told of others being thrown from the upper floors of the building.

During this attack, many students were killed on the spot, hundreds were brutally beaten, and many were arrested and later imprisoned. To better understand the vicious actions taken on the student protesters by the Basij militia, read the following firsthand account of one student protester of the July 9, 1999, demonstration. Javid Tehrani tells about his life since the events of that day:

Eight years have passed since plain clothed police officers attacked and invaded the student dormitories at Tehran University. During that night, Ezat Ebrahim Nejad and tens of other students were murdered at the hands of Iranian Regime's barbaric agents. Thousands of student activists were arrested and subjected to the most brutal tortures imaginable. Manouchehr Mohammadi, a student activist and a freedom fighter, lost his younger brother, Akbar Mohammadi, under torture in Evin Prison. Eight years later, I am still in prison in relation to my activities during the July 9, 1999 (18 Tir) student demonstrations.

Eight years ago without having committed any crime, without a lawyer, and without due process, I was sentenced to 8 years of imprisonment. After having served 4 years and without any request on my part, I was pardoned by the supreme leader and released. I was released exactly 43 days after my mother's death. While my mom was ill, I had requested to visit her briefly in the hospital on her deathbed, and later when she passed away, I requested to attend her funeral; however, both my requests were denied.

I was re-arrested shortly after my release once without any evidence and solely for my human rights activities. The Intelligence Ministry decided I was not deserving of the pardon and I must serve the remaining 4 years of my prison term as well as be sentenced to 74 lashes on my back. It is unfair that my back must pay the price for my mind and my hands. On this 8th anniversary of July 9, 1999 (18 Tir), demonstrations, besides keeping the memory of that day alive and remembering what happened to the innocent students, I ask all human right activists and organizations to identify and remember all student activists who have become faceless and forgotten in Iranian prisons and take the steps necessary to help them.

Viva Iran

Javid Tehrani

This was a letter written by Tehrani and mailed from prison. In hopes to get the word out, he has asked for his personal story to be reposted on blogs and shared with people around the world.

DAYS THAT FOLLOWED

T he protest at Tehran University on July 9, 1999, was just the beginning. The brutal student attacks ignited the fuse of the student population's passion for democracy and recognition of human rights. The days that followed the infamous attack were filled with acts of dissidence towards the Clerical Regime. Infuriated, the protesters began lashing out at the government, verbally and physically. Public property was destroyed by masses of students that seemed to take over the streets of the city. Chants scrutinizing the actions of the supreme leader and clerics could be heard at all hours of the day. Students gathered in large groups and protested in the form of "sit-ins."

This passionate response to the unjust actions of the Iranian government lasted with a high level of intensity for a number of days. Concerned about the image of the country and the opposition's chaotic behavior, the government attempted to squash all reform efforts. This attempt to restore "peace" was facilitated by the Basij militia. The Basij swept the cities of Iran and once again put a stop to dissidence by the use of coercive force.

In the same interview previously referred to, Mehran Adib tells more about his party's involvement in the student uprisings. He said the reason for the Islamic Republic being so against his party is due to the fact that they suspect other countries control this party and its activities. The authorities of the Clerical Regime have pointed their fingers at the Iranian People's Party for causing these uprisings.

When asked what his party's involvement was in the 1999 student demonstrations, Mehran Adib said, "The demonstrations for freedom of the press and against the attack against the student residence hall were organized by the Mellat-e party in the first days. Then the government sent the Anzar Hisbollah, militant Islamic thugs who are responsible for the escalation of the peaceful demonstrations. The excesses were supposed to provide an excuse for the brutal suppression of the democratic movement. We are against all violence. But now the government is trying to give us the blame for the chaos."

The abominable Basij forces were too aggressive for the citizens to put up a fight. Unfortunately, the resistance displayed by the reformists was quickly stifled. President Khatami's efforts to create change from within still looked promising in the eyes of the desperate Iranians. The "student population" continued to rally support regarding reform within the country. Their main concerns were the recognition of their human rights (mostly in regards to censorship and free press) and the separation of church and state. They knew that their ideal government couldn't exist without separating church and state.

Not surprisingly, Minister of Interior Abdullah Mousavi-Lari declared that the student demonstrations had taken place without ministry authorization. Senior Tehran police chiefs were charged with responsibility for allowing the raid, although the head of Tehran's police department, Hedayat Lotfian, was exonerated. In mid-August 1999, a hard-hitting report by the National Security Council criticized the police and conservative militia groups, and President Khatami declared that "police officers and non-military personnel" were responsible for the raid, but no public criminal proceedings were instituted. The full story of who ordered the raid and which forces carried it out remain shrouded in mystery.

After 6 days of protest, the supreme leader was determined to put a stop to any sign of dissidence. The demonstrators' push for President Khatami to stand up to theocracy was immediately shattered. Khatami suddenly released a statement that supported the supreme leader's call for all demonstrations to be stopped immediately and indefinitely. The decision made by Khatami, in support of the supreme leader, was a heavy blow to the Iranian population. The only person with enough power to potentially spark change in Iran's government system had now seemed to turn on the very people who elected him president.

Students have continued to get the word our regarding the 1999 student uprisings. They are desperate to alert the world of the violations of their human rights in the crudest of ways. Amnesty International has continued their support for the student protestors by encouraging the government to bring those responsible to justice, but despite their efforts, not much has been done. As you will see, this is frighteningly similar to what is happening today.

CHAPTER 5

THE FACE OF THE 1999 STUDENT UPRISINGS

If the 1999 student uprising had one concrete effect on Iranian society, it would be the young Iranian leaders that it formed. Sam Ghandchi states, "[The students] were the new leaders who had come out of the July 9th, 1999, students' movement, leaders who were neither with Mujahidin nor with monarchy. They were an independent new force that Iranian progressive aspirations had created, and they were getting stronger and stronger, and the attacks of the regime's vigilantes would only make this force more aware as to how to form a democratic futurist Iran."

"I wish each and every Iranian could travel abroad, come to the U.S. or go to Europe for just one week, and feel, smell, and breathe freedom, human dignity, and realize the value of their lives."

—Ahmed Batebi
1999 Student activist

Ahmed Batebi, whose only wish was to be a photojournalist, was a film student attending the

University of Tehran. It was during his time at the university that Ahmed Batebi became a human rights activist. He is most known for his internationally recognized picture on July 17, 1999, cover of the *Economist* magazine, where he is holding up a shirt splattered with the blood of another protestor. The photo itself has since been called "an icon for Iran's student reform movement." It was that photo that would become a symbol for the world, and the same photo that would become a source of pain for years to come.

Batebi was attending a protest on the campus on July 9, 1999, when the attack occurred. News that the student-run newspaper was to be shut down by court order spread through the campus. The students who dreamed of a better Iran put their hopes and dreams into the *Salam* creation. When the paper was to be canceled, the students took to the streets, and Batebi was among the protestors. Within minutes of the protest, the Basij militia, under the orders of the Islamic Republic, stormed the campus. In the ensuing riot, police fired into a crowd of unarmed students. A bullet hit a wall behind Batebi and ricocheted past his head into his friend's shoulder standing next to him. Ahmed Batebi told *60 Minutes* that it sounded as if a bee buzzed past his head. His friend fell to the ground. Trying to do the right thing, Ahmed Batebi leapt into action and tried to help. He took his shirt off and used it to apply pressure to the wound. After he could not get the bleeding to stop, another protestor helped him take his friend to the medical center.

Ahmed Batebi immediately returned, waving the now-infamous shirt, trying to show the world what the police had done. It was the photo taken of Ahmed waving his shirt that would forever change his life. Just days after a picture of the shirt was released to the public, Ahmed Batebi was arrested. It is his story of the events after being arrested that would become a source of courage, perseverance, and the undying will to stand for what is right.

Although officially, Iran denies ever having political prisoners, stories such as that of Ahmed Batebi find their way to the light every day. Ahmed Batebi was taken into custody following the protest and held for years with no trial until his escape last year. He told *60 Minutes* he was taken to a "special" prison strictly for interrogation, where he was held for several months in solitary confinement. After the seventh month, he was blindfolded and taken from the prison. He didn't know where he was going; he just assumed it was all part of the questioning.

Once he had reached his destination, his blindfold was removed. All Ahmed Batebi could see was the faint outline of a judge, and the picture that would come to haunt him. Ahmed Batebi said the judge held up the picture and told him, "With this picture, you have signed your own death sentence; you have defaced the face of the Islamic Republic that is a representation of God on earth. You have defaced it around the world, and therefore, you have to be put to death." They wanted Ahmed Batebi to betray his fellow protestors and lie to the world. However, Batebi refused to do that or betray his fellow student activists despite all the threats.

It took less than three minutes for his trial. He was judged and convicted in less time than it takes to read this. Then he was transferred and held at Evin Prison, deep in the heart of Iran. Ahmed Batebi told *60 Minutes* that he spent another 17 months in solitary confinement—in a cell that is not much bigger than the average bathtub. They kept a bright light on 24 hours a day. He was completely isolated with no contact, and even worse, he had no information of the outside world. All he knew for 17 months was his cell and the bright light above him that would never turn off. After a while, he developed insomnia. It affected him emotionally, more so than physically. The guards then began to increase their torture. They made sure he did not sleep for long periods of time, and this sleep deprivation started to drive him mad.

"I hadn't slept for maybe 72 hours. I couldn't think clearly. I was drooling. I wanted to sleep, but they would slap me to keep me awake. In the final hours when even the slapping wouldn't keep me up, they cut my arms and hands and put salt in my wounds so the burning would keep me awake."

They didn't stop with the sleep deprivation. When he still refused to betray his fellow students, he was beaten. He was once kicked so hard in the mouth he lost three teeth. He was beaten with cables on the bottom of his feet and back. They beat him all while he was in solitary confinement. He never knew when his cell door would open and he would be tortured or which technique they would use. It was this fear and the sense of never sleeping that almost drove him crazy. On a few occasions, his tormentors even beat his testicles.

On top of the numerous beatings he suffered, he was also tortured mentally and psychologically as well. Ahmed Batebi says there was toilet in a corner of the interrogation room that was filled with human feces. On more than one occasion, his head was held down in the toilet, where his face would be covered in feces. On some occasions, he wished for death. He never knew when tormentors would return to torture him. Yet, he never betrayed his fellow protestors regardless of the torment and his wish for death.

As if he hadn't suffered enough, one day, he heard his mother's voice coming from the cell next to him. At the time, he didn't know it was just a recording. The only question he could possible ask himself is what is his mother doing in a place like this—a place so dark, covered in dried blood, a place filled with pain.

> *"I would hear her voice. And I would say in this place, where there's all this torture and all this pain, they've arrested my mother also. And maybe she's in the prison cell next to me or across from me. And, of course, this really bothered me a lot."*

Just when he didn't think he could take anymore, he was taken into a room with ropes hanging from the ceiling and three stools directly under them. He was tied, bound, and led to the center stool. To his left, a prisoner was also led, and to the right, a man was also being led up the stool. They were told that this was the time that was set for their execution and then a noose was put around their neck. I could only imagine what thoughts must have gone through their mind as they prepared for the end. As time went by, one guard kicked the stool from underneath the left man, and another from the right. They immediately fell. However, their necks did not snap. Ahmed Batebi had to watch as they slowly suffocated to death. He could see their toes curl as the fought for oxygen. Ahmed said their feet started to turn blue before they simply stopped moving and began to swing lifelessly.

"They made me stand on a stool. Two other people were on stools, one to my left, and one to my right. And they put a rope around our necks. And they said, 'You have a death sentence and you will be executed.' And then they kicked away the other two stools. The other two people were hanging, and their feet turned blue, and they died. I was still on my stool. I was shaking all over."

Although I have given you an accurate account of the torture Ahmed Batebi had to experience, I could never do his story justice. He had to endure this miserable existence for years. Ahmed was once a simple film student who dreamt of becoming a journalist. He wanted to take pictures that would inspire a world; he never imagined that it would be a picture of him that truly inspired the world.

CHAPTER 6 ۶

2000 PRESIDENTIAL ELECTIONS

After 3 years of swelling pressure between reformers and conservatives, the result was the key. The election proved to be an echoing approval for change. Three-quarters of the seats were won by a large coalition of reformers and their independent allies. Thirty-eight of the forty seats apportioned to the capital went to reformers in Tehran. For President Mohammad Khatami, it also meant tightly placed in the hands of reformers were two of the three divisions of government, the executive and legislative.

"In this election, people were asking for their legal rights and we now want to restore those basics, including freedom of speech, press and privacy; the right to go to court, to have a lawyer, the assumption of innocence until proven guilty and a ban on torture; a ban on censorship, surveillance or listening to conversations; and the universal right to housing, free education and free health care," Khatami said firmly.

The supreme leader openly sanctioned the assault on the press. Speaking at Friday prayers on April 22, 2000, Ayatollah Khamenei characterized the press as a "stronghold of Western influence" in Iran. He defended the newspaper closures by saying, "We are trying to stop the enemy from realizing his propaganda conspiracy." President Khatami was far less direct, simply hinting that conservatives were exploiting religious values to increase their grip on power.

At the same time, Khatami was careful to distance himself from some of the independent media, whose content, he warned, signified an unacceptable "shift towards secularism" in Iran.

In December 2000, advocates of greater press freedom suffered a further blow when Minister of Culture and Islamic Guidance Ayatollah Mohajerani resigned. He was seen as the main guiding hand behind efforts to liberalize and increase press freedom and had been repeatedly challenged to resign by conservatives. In 1999, he escaped an attempt to impeach him only by making an impassioned and eloquent defense of press freedom on the floor of the parliament. Mohajerani's departure from office represented for many the end of the period in which the independent print media had been able to act as the public voice of the reform movement. He had worked with diminishing success from within the system to safeguard an independent voice for the press.

As press closures and arrests of journalists continued, reformists appealed to the rule of law. Deputy Minister of Culture and Islamic Guidance for Press Affairs Shaban Shahidi stated on August 19, "It would be ideal if no publication is shut down before going to trial, and that no journalist or managing director would be arrested without an open trial in front of a jury." He also stated that reopening some of the closed newspapers "could help calm down the atmosphere in the country." President Khatami finally spoke out on the press clamp down on August 21, 2000, at a televised news conference. "The situation which has come about nowadays for our press and mass media is not satisfactory," he said.

Attacks on the press and on journalists continued in 2001. In January, the authorities closed the philosophical and cultural monthly *Kiyan*. The journal had published academic articles debating the philosophical underpinnings of the reform movement. Among the journalists most recently detained are Fariba Davoodi-Mohajer, arrested on February 18, and Mohammad Vali Beig, head of the *Jame-e Rouz* publishing society. On February 28,

2001, journalist Massoud Behnoud was sentenced to 19 months of imprisonment for "spreading untruths and insulting the Islamic system." Two independent journalists, Hoda Saber and Reza Alijani, were taken into detention in March 2001, and as of late May, were still being held in an unknown location.

A PRELUDE TO THE "GREEN MOVEMENT"

"The Iranians are suffering from the policies in the last four years, they have been humiliated all over the world and I really feel sorry for these people."

—Mir-Hossein Mousavi

The last 4 years (2005–2009) have been worse than ever for Iranian citizens due to the reign of President Mahmoud Ahmadinejad. Historically, most presidents have acted as "counterweights" to the extreme ideologies of the supreme leader, but unfortunately, Ahmadinejad made those ideologies even more of a reality for the people of Iran by echoing them. Angry at the previous 4 years of Ahmadinejad's presidency, Iranians, mainly the student population, were determined to stop the reelection of Ahmadinejad in the 2009 election. (In Iran, the presidential term is 4 years in length and a person can only serve two consecutive terms.)

Iranian society has changed dramatically over the past 30 years and bears little resemblance either to the expectations of or the picture painted by the leadership of the Islamic Republic. Indeed, as much as the ruling clerics like to project self-confidence and the ability to predict the future, they could not have envisaged a society with these characteristics. While many of these surprising developments have occurred because of the policies of the Islamic Republic, others have occurred despite or regardless of them. If our picture of Iran prior to 1979 was so positive that we could not imagine anything negative happening inside the country, our picture of Iran today is so negative that we cannot imagine anything positive taking place. Yet, as this essay shows, some government policies have been pragmatic and beneficial to society.

The "demographic gift" of the post revolutionary period has resulted in a doubling of the population to 71 million, and more specifically, a burgeoning of the youth population. Two out of three Iranians are under the age of 30. As reflected by Iran's 85 percent literacy rate (among the highest of Muslim countries), young Iranians are much better educated than previous generations. However, fewer than one in three can remember the revolution, and the young suffer disproportionately from the regime's failures. In 2007, by the government's own reckoning, nearly every other Iranian between the ages of 25 and 29 was unemployed. A lack of jobs is no doubt one reason for the prevalence of crime and delinquency in the country.

The demographic surge has been accompanied by rapid urbanization; seven out of ten Iranians now live in cities. Large cities are confronted with serious issues regarding municipal management of basic services, poor planning for housing construction, and serious environmental risks. The population of Tehran has increased to 14 million (from six million in 1980). The World Bank, which in 2003 lent Tehran $20 million to clean up the air, said the pollution in Iran's major cities exceeded World Health Organization standards by 40 percent to 340 percent.

Iranian society is a nominally austere society and much of its actual behavior attests to the fact that the regime's draconian policies of imposing Islamic restrictions on everything, ranging from the country's penal code to university admission policies, have backfired. According to one source, Iranian clergy have complained that more than 70 percent of the population does not perform their daily prayers and that less than 2 percent attend Friday mosques. The rise of lay intellectuals, such as Abdolkarim Soroush, is due to the fact that their argument emphasizes the separation of religion from politics in Iran, implicitly hinting at the problems caused by clerical involvement in politics.

Iranian society has become globalized. A recent blog census found that there are more than 700,000 weblogs written in Persian, compared with about 50 in neighboring Iraq. Iranian bloggers include members of Hizbullah, teenagers in Tehran, retirees in Los Angeles, religious students in Qom, dissident journalists who left Iran a few years ago, exiles who left 30 years ago, current members of the Majlis (parliament), reformist politicians, a multitude of poets, and—quite famously—the president of Iran, among many others. This has allowed the Internet-savvy Iranian youth to have access to a wide range of perspectives that criticize the Islamic Republic's policy positions.

The number of women graduating from Iran's universities is overtaking the number of men, promising a change in the job market and, with it, profound social change. Well over half of the university students in Iran are now women. In the applied Physics Department of Azad University, 70 percent of the graduates are women—a statistic which would make many universities in the West proud. Ten years ago, only 12.5 percent of Iranian medical students were women, and the government responded by setting a goal that half of all new students would be female. Today, one-third of the 22,326 students in Iran's 38 medical schools are women. But the regime's policy of depriving female doctors of training in male hospital wards leads to tensions. In 2001, students at the Fatimieh Female Medical School in Qom, one of Iran's most religious cities, held a sit-in protest in Tehran.

Striking a balance between the republican and Islamic components of governance has become exceedingly complicated, if not confounding. Iran has a confusing legal structure that is based on parliamentary legislations, codification of Islamic law into an Islamic penal code, religious rulings of *mujtahids* (fatwas), opinions of the late Ayatollah Ruhollah Khomeini (known as the *faqih* or jurisconsult), and rulings by the current supreme leader, Ali Khamenei (*vali amr moslemin*). Although republicanism is expressed in elections for a president, parliamentary deputies, and city councils, powerful unelected clerical bodies, such as the Council of Guardians, use their authority to veto any candidate that they view as "unacceptable." Moreover, according to Article 167 of the Iranian Constitution, "Whenever there is no law or the law is ambiguous, judges must refer to authoritative sources and authentic fatwas." This has led to thousands of contradictory fatwas, which makes it impossible for judges to give uniform rulings on similar violations.

The publication of books by nonclerics directly question and challenge the clerics on their interpretation of Islamic law. To cite one example, Emad Baghi's book, *Right to Life*, argues for the abolition and suspension of the death penalty in Iran and draws on Qur'anic verses to argue that, "Crime, felony, and executions are the results of and contributors to a culture of violence."

As much as the ruling élite in the Islamic Republic has had a difficult time negotiating the boundaries of Islamic principles with its republican constitutionalism, they have not been as rigid in finding a positive interpretation of Shari'a when it comes to the role of science, particularly regarding important scientific discoveries. Since the late 1990s, Iranian scientists have engaged the religious hierarchy in a lively debate on genetic engineering, biomedical sciences, and ethical issues. Iran is now investing heavily in science after decades of neglect. Even Supreme Leader Ayatollah 'Ali Khamene'i has issued a fatwa calling on researchers to secure Iran's position as the "leader in science" in the Middle East over the next 20 years. They have effectively applied the principle of *maslahat* (expediency) as a way of justifying important scientific discoveries since there are no texts in the Qur'an or Sunna that expressly prohibit such innovations. Iranians have been quite open in their judgments about scientific developments in genetic engineering, artificial insemination, in vitro fertilization (IVF), and transplants. This is in contrast to the controversy that has been raging for decades about kidney transplants in Egypt.

Iranians from all walks of life crave stability on their borders and a government that can deliver on its promises and plans. After living in a state of semicrisis for 30 years, Iranians have learned their lessons about revolution, the consequences of mixing religion with politics, and the costs of living in a country that is under sanctions and pressures. With 30 percent inflation, a 35 percent increase in food prices in 2008, a $50 billion deficit, and an unemployment rate of 16 percent (the highest level since the 1960s), Iran's rulers will have a hard time convincing the population that they are better off in 2009.

AHMADINEJAD'S UNSUCCESSFUL TERM

Iran entered into the tenth presidential election in difficult socioeconomic conditions. The overwhelming majority of the Iranian working classes were suffering from unprecedented hardship and poverty during the 4 years of Ahmadinejad's government and hard-line policies. Examination of the policies revealed the specific characteristics of the route taken by Ahmadinejad's administration, affiliated with grand mercantile capitalism and the bureaucratic bourgeoisie of the country. This affected some of the reasons behind the people's mass movement against this reactionary regime. The primary direction of the socioeconomic policies of Ahmadinjad's government and some of its penalties can be summarized as follows:

The economy of Iran, and the direction in which it should travel, has been a debate between the fundamentalists and the reformists groups since the day the Islamic Republic took over in 1979. When the Islamic Republic was established, one of their first major political accomplishments was the addition of Article 44 to its penal code. (According to Article 44, the Iranian economy consists of three sectors: the state, cooperative, and private sectors, but all large-scale and mother industries of the country are entirely owned by the state. This article was amended to allow for privatization.)

Following an executive order issued by the supreme leader of the regime, it was revoked by Ahmadinjad's government. The effect of these policies is to bring the macropolicies of the regime into line with the policies and prescriptions of the IMF and World Bank; this was already tried in various countries. The unsuccessful consequences of these policies could be visibly observed in the developing countries of the world. The supreme leader in 2007 gave an executive order regarding Article 44 that was cordially welcomed by the IMF.

The IMF stated, "Lately, the government has been pursuing privatization more seriously," in a report about the economic prospects of Iran. Ayatollah Khamenei issued an executive order regarding Article 44 of the constitution that more than 80 percent of state-owned enterprises must be privatized in the next 10 years. This executive order rejuvenated privatization plans. Privatization of state-owned enterprises is to be completed by the end of the 5-year plan.

Mounting Foreign Debts and Destruction of National   Production

A damaging domestic production and a swelling Iranian debt have allowed another key political decision by Ahmadinjad's government, and this has given an opening for domestic markets to import consumer goods more than ever before. In the first 4 months of the current Iranian year, from spring of 2008, the import of luxury consumer goods like cars, fully automatic washing machines, fridges, cigarettes, audio equipment, decorations, cosmetics, and the like, has significantly increased according to reports published by Iran's customs (this is in parallel to the increase in value and weight of imported industrial raw material as a result of the imposed sanctions).

Iran's foreign debt not only failed to decrease during Ahmadinejad's term, but soared at an increasing rate, this being another important economic indicator despite the enormous increase in oil profits. On March 9, 2008, the *Kargozaran* newspaper quoted the ISNA that wrote: "The Business Monitor International stated in its latest report that Iran's foreign debts would increase in excess of $8 billion in 4 years. BMI projected Iran's foreign debt in the last year at $23.3 billion, as reported in the 2nd quarter report of 2008, which would increase by $500 million this year to reach $24 billion. It is believed by BMI that Iran's foreign debts in the coming years will grow; in [Iranian] years 1387 (2008) and 1388 (2009) it will increase to $26.3 and $28.1 billion, and going along the same increasing trend, it will soar to $29.2 billion in 1389 (2010)."

Growing Mass Hardship and Poverty

It is very hard to find accurate and acceptable statistics documenting poverty in Iran. Thus, one has to read between the lines. A concrete conclusion can be reached that poverty and destitution have increased in severity during Ahmadinejad's government. Recent studies by the Central Bank (of Iran) have shown that the number of people living under the poverty threshold increased from 18 percent to 19 percent during the first 2 years of the ninth government.

Currently, between 14 and 15 million people are living under the poverty line based on these figures. Ali Asgari, the Economic Deputy of President Office of Planning and Strategic Control, stated, "about 20 percent of the population lives under the poverty line according to the published economic index. The dimensions of the escalation of poverty and unemployment are more distinct when inflation and the rise of the cost of living are considered. The price of some food items shows an increase of 40 to 45% in just about a month as reported this summer by the Central Bank of the regime."

Working Class Under Attack

In a large meeting in December of 2008 held by our party's Central Committee, of topic were the issues listed above and particular attention was given to the plight of the working class and the increasing attacks of the regime against progressive forces. The documentation of the meeting is as follows:

"The harsh living conditions of the working people will produce a growing dissatisfaction and opposition among them. Last year witnessed were tons of labour protest movements, demonstrations by educational workers, vast protest movements by students and a continuance that women of the struggle have against the government and its policies.

"Thus being, Iran's working class was faced with a hard challenge last year. The fight against temporary contracts is one of the most important arenas of the trade struggle among the workers, which were promoted by Ahmadinejad's administration and anti-labour ministry of labour and have had an unparallel growth. Temporary contracts consist of 80% of workers in factories and in manufacturing industries, as per statistics released earlier this year. These contracts usually cover a working term of 2 months and 10 days up to 6 months.

"A large portion of these contract workers are working under the most harsh slavery conditions. This has had an adverse impact on the efforts of labour activists, permitting them to form and support independent labour organizations. In the past few months, Ahmadinejad's administration and the reactions that parliament have started talking about changes to the Labour Law and taking away the rights of workers. Labour organizations and activists have quickly reacted to the attitude given by parliament.

"Our party has repeatedly stressed that scattering among workers and labour movements, for whatever reason, slow down the growth of the trade union movement in the country and ultimately will give the regime a chance to divide the struggles of the workers and suppress them one by one. Arrests and brutal and suppressive action from the security forces of the regime have dampened the efforts of the labour activists to form independent labour organizations, with ever increasing difficulty."

Conclusion of Our Party's Meeting:

"Parallel to having adopted anti-popular economic and social policies, the regime, faced with the dissatisfaction of the masses across the country trying to prevent harmonization and synchronization of protests of working people, escalation of these protests have intensified its pressure and suppression policies. But continuing pressures and organized attacks against The Syndicate of Workers of the Tehran and Suburban Bus (Vahad) Company and keeping Mansour Osanloo [chair of its board] in custody in the regime's torture chambers, and also increasing the activities of suppression forces constant in the Islamic Associations of Labour, and an increase in firing labour activists all being a part of policies that the regime are pursuing in order to contain the movement in the country. Equally enforced against the student movement and the women's movement are the suppressive policies of the regime which are not limited to the labour movement. The student movement, within the last year, was faced with extensive confrontation by the regime's security forces."

Imperialist Intervention and Iran's Democratic Movement

One of the goals of the great Iranian Revolution of 1979 was to put an end to the U.S.-British intervention in our country's affairs, for Iran has had a long and painful history of imperialist intervention. The world has witnessed the continuous stand-off between the Bush administration and the Iranian regime for many years.

In the final year of the Bush presidency, with a growing threat of military intervention in Iran by U.S. imperialism, the progressive forces in Iran joined the growing social forces in mobilizing a nationwide peace movement comprising of the national democratic and progressive forces. Systematically suppressed by the regime, this peace movement was aimed to mobilize against the risk of war and the U.S. attack against Iran. This movement encompassed largely the same forces which are currently fighting the regime against the election frauds, which includes a relatively wide spectrum of political forces, the women's movement, the students' movement, and the labour movement.

It is also important to restate that the growing tension and imperialist interventionist policies against Iran were supposedly linked to Iran's nuclear policy. It is essential to restate that the issue of the nuclear tensions and the resulting international tensions have led to issuing a number of resolutions by the security council of the UN against Iran.

Human Rights Report Under Ahmadinejad's Presidency

The number of occurrences and methods used in violating human rights has greatly increased during Ahmadinejad's presidential term. The violation of human rights within Iran has become such an epidemic that Human Rights Watch has released a report blaming Ahmadinejad's administration for the escalation of this issue. In their report, "Iran: Rights Crisis Escalates, Faces and Cases from Ahmadinejad's Crackdown," Human Rights Watch concluded that Iran must immediately do the following:

> • Stop all executions of juvenile offenders and abolish the death penalty for juvenile offenders;
>
> • Release all political prisoners and persons jailed solely for exercising peacefully their right to freedom of expression, association, and assembly;

• Honor Iran's standing invitations to the UN Special Rapporteurs and allow international human-rights organizations to visit Iran to conduct research and advocacy.

During President Ahmadinejad's administration, Iran's human rights record has reached new lows. The security and intelligence services controlled by his administration have led an ever-expanding crackdown against peaceful activists and dissidents. Hard-line elements within the judiciary, emboldened by Ahmadinejad's lack of concern for human rights violations, have sent the number of executions skyrocketing, including those of juvenile offenders. In addition to the prosecution and imprisonment of peaceful activists, Ahmadinejad's presidency has also created an intense atmosphere of fear and intimidation across most sectors of the country's once-vibrant and growing civil society. The human cost of Ahmadinejad's policies is registering a heavy toll on Iran's civil society. It is imperative for the international community to take up the opportunity of President Ahmadinejad's presence at the United Nations to voice its concerns about the increasingly grave human rights violations in Iran.

LEAD UP TO THE 2009 ELECTIONS

The student population of Iran seemed to heavily support one particular presidential candidate from the beginning, Mir-Hossein Mousavi, in hopes that he would defeat Ahmadinejad, now infamous in the eyes of the Iranian citizens. The massive amount of support that Mousavi seemed to instantly gain wasn't a surprise to many. With this being said, it is often questioned whether Mousavi has gained the amount of support that he has because of his ability to deliver what he promises, or rather because the only other choice is another 4 years of Ahmadinejad.

On June 1, 2009, *Newsweek* featured "Anyone but Ahmadinejad" as their cover story. The author, Maziar Bahari, writes, "If Ahmadinejad wins, that means the end of this reformist dream for a while. Many of these young people will be depressed and even leave the country. But if Mousavi wins, that means the citizens have won despite Ahmadinejad's deceitful policies and the support he receives from above." One can clearly see that Mousavi entered the presidential election with an advantage; Iranians had already suffered for 4 years under Ahmadinejad.

Mousavi's involvement in regards to government of the Islamic Republic can be traced back to the 1979 revolution, which resulted in the Shah being overthrown. Shortly after the revolution of 1979, Mousavi was appointed to and assumed the position of prime minister of Iran. He filled this position for the next 8 years, but in 1989, the position was abolished by the Islamic Republic. At that time, Mousavi reverted to what some would call political exile. The political direction in which the Islamic Republic had moved left Mousavi disheartened and discouraged. It was at this time that he reverted to his passion of architecture and teaching.

Mousavi couldn't stay out of the political shadows forever. Nearly 20 years after dismissing himself from politics, he was vetted by the Guardian Council as a candidate in the 2009 presidential election. Many people have wondered why Mousavi would even submit himself to this overwhelmingly controversial presidential race. What on his agenda made him jump headfirst into this corrupt and divided government? The answer is simply one man—Khatami.

Mohammad Khatami, Ahmadinejad's predecessor and a man praised by some Iranians for his fight for human rights, had actually entered the 2009 presidential race. After continued threats of assassination and advice from the supreme leader that he should withdraw his candidacy, Khatami had no choice but to withdraw. This still doesn't answer the question of how Mousavi came to be the overwhelmingly acclaimed and "chosen" candidate of the Iranian people.

On March 17, 2009, the Guardian issued a news article announcing Mohammad Khatami's announcement to withdraw from the presidential campaign. They included this quote from Khatami: "Despite the difference in our opinions and actions, the important thing is that [Mousavi] … seriously defends and will defend the fundamental rights and freedoms [of people] and … the country's international reputation." This was all that was needed to push Mousavi to the front-runner position of the race. All of Khatami's loyal supporters instantly found themselves actively, and enthusiastically, supporting the Mousavi campaign.

By quickly announcing his political platform to the public, Mousavi immediately became the front-runner for the activists, including the student population. He decided that he would be the one that would act as much more than a simple "counterweight" to the Islamic Republic.

Instantly, Mousavi's campaign gained immense support from the student population; just over 70 percent of the Iranian population. As the months progressed leading up to the presidential election, Mousavi's support was overwhelming. Not only did he have the majority of Iranian citizens supporting him, but they were also the ones that were more likely to vocalize their opinion concerning their candidate. By the beaming energy that Mousavi ignited throughout the country as a whole, it was obvious that the people had already chosen their future president.

Seeing the enthusiasm that the student population was displaying in support of Mousavi's campaign, the Clerical Regime felt that there would be chaos and disagreement in regards to the results of the election. In hopes to put a stop to any dissident organization by the students, the Iranian government had the SMS feature disabled on all cell phones in the country. The Clerical Regime knew that the populace would organize themselves through SMS messages sent from their mobile phones and it would make their stand that much stronger. The Clerical Regime learned of the power that these mobile phones held after seeing the effective use of Twitter in the preelection campaigns. In addition to disabling the SMS feature, the Clerical Regime also restricted the use of the Internet, foreign news media, and reporters.

JUNE 12, 2009: ELECTION DAY

This was thought to be just yet another typical presidential election in Iran. The only thing that seemed to appear different in this election is the fact that a reform candidate, Mousavi, was actually vetted by the Guardian Council. Going back to the structure of the Iranian government, all Iranian presidential candidates must be approved by the Guardian Council before they can officially launch their presidential campaign. Through this "filtering" process, the Guardian Council gives itself the authority to keep "radicals" from running for president, totally defeating the purpose of a "democratic" election.

The citizens of Iran have had their own differing opinions concerned with who should be the new president, and it has historically been divided between the urban and rural areas. In Iran, it seems that the city dwellers tend to be more politically liberal, while those that reside in the country lean more towards the conservative side. It's more or less the same scenario that has been seen in nearly every country in the world.

The election polls opened at 8:00 a.m. and after the supreme leader, Ayatollah Khamenei, cast his vote at a mosque in southern Tehran, he praised the public for their enthusiasm and noted how many people were waiting to vote. He praised them for their awareness of the situation. He never actually endorsed any candidate, but he did give a description of the "perfect" president. This description was very much like Ahmadinejad.

Much speculation came from the streets as to who would win the election. Some said the election would be rigged in favor of Ahmadinejad. Some wondered if it would be a close race, if some voters would be swayed toward Ahmadinejad by coercion. Iran's election rules state that if no candidate won more than 50 percent of the vote, the top two candidates would run against each other in a runoff the following Friday. Many thought this would happen because of the astonishing support Mousavi had amassed.

One reason for the crowds being so large, besides the obvious support for Mousavi by Iranian youth, was because this day was a holiday and no one had to work. This could work in both candidates' favor. The masses of people coming to vote caused voting hours to be extended four times during the day.

As if the political atmosphere weren't tense enough, while the votes were being counted, presidential candidate Mousavi claimed publicly that he had won the election. At roughly the same time, the state announced Ahmadinejad as the new president of Iran.

At 5:10 this evening, reports started pouring in to journalists that text messaging had been blocked. It is believed that this action was a deliberate attempt to squash out the opposition's influence on the media. Al Jazeera reports:

> "Iran state broadcaster IRIB keeps tight control of what's seen and heard on the air waves here, but the reformists say it's always been against them....The Internet has been a key weapon for the reformists."

Press TV is a government-sponsored satellite news channel. At 4:30 p.m., Press TV reported that the official preliminary election results show that Mahmoud Ahmadinejad had a lead, holding a little over 69 percent of the ballots. The briefing provided by the Iranian Election Commission chief came as a surprise to many and caused a lot of people to wonder if this "surprise announcement" was yet another tactic to suppress the talk of oppositional wins. This happened only 2 hours after the polls closed, causing suspicion of fraud.

Mousavi urged the supreme leader to intervene in the situation because of the voter irregularities. He insisted that there had not been enough ballots in some areas where his supporters were dominant.

Supporters of Ahmadinejad were already celebrating in the streets, while others who supported Mousavi were crying foul. Women openly wept while others complained bitterly and vowed to do something about it. It was expected the opposition supporters would take to the streets in protest, even though Ahmadreza Radan, deputy commander of the Iranian National Police, warned them not to. Police began to strategize how to control the situation at hand and donned their riot gear as they headed out to the streets.

Before the elections, many suspected Ahmadinejad of limiting the opposition's voice. He is in sole control of the country's media. This occurrence solidified many Iranians' opinions that a true democratic election process was never intended.

DEMONSTRATIONS IN THE STREETS

At 8:00 a.m. the Iranian media announced that 18 million votes went to Ahmadinejad and 9 million went to Mousavi. About 250,000 votes each went to the other two candidates, Mehdi Karroubi and Mohsen Rezai.

Protestors against the success of Ahmadinejad and those celebrating that victory poured into the streets. Intense demonstrations brought the Iranian police, who used batons and tear gas to stop the clash that followed. Demonstrators declared Ahmadinejad stole the election. It was reported that at least one person had been shot in Vanak Square in Tehran and automobiles were overturned and burned in the street.

Mousavi stated that he rejected the election results and encouraged supporters to fight them, but he also urged them to be calm and patient. He did not appear the rest of the day and many thought he may have been arrested. Ayatollah Khamenei did not give heed to pleas for intervention or appeals. He just congratulated Ahmadinejad and asked the other candidates to give him their support.

More demonstrators took to the streets of Tehran during the afternoon. Women, youth, students, and members of the moderate clerical establishment turned out in the thousands, chanting and wearing the bright green campaign colors of Mousavi. Tehran wasn't the only city seeing this kind of unrest. Because of the activities, all universities were closed, cell phone transmissions remained blocked, and many Web sites were shut down for a second day.

The government vehemently proclaimed that the vote had not been rigged. That although Mousavi had a great deal of support from students and other youth in the city of Tehran, he had little support from the people outside of the city. Rumors flew that for every 3,000 votes for Mousavi, only 1,000 were counted. It was said that the government had been planning fraud for weeks prior to the election. There was also talk that the ballots had been misleading. Voters had to fill in the code for the candidate they wished to win. The Number 4 was for Ahmadinejad and Number 44 was for Mousavi.

UNREST CONTINUES

Violence continued in Tehran on Sunday. Rumors continued to fly regarding the election, and it was thought that over 100 opposition members had been detained by the police. Riots also were prevalent in other Iranian cities, and demonstrations took place in Washington, D.C., and European capitals.

The Association of Combatant Clergy released a statement on reformist Web sites, proclaiming that the vote was fixed and called for a new election. They also stated that they were afraid the people of Iran would lose confidence in the system. Even Mehdi Karroubi, another candidate in the election for position of president, agreed with Mousavi's demand that the election be declared null and void on opposition Web sites. He stated he did not recognize Ahmadinejad as president.

As if to quell all resistance, Ahmadinejad spoke in Valiasr Square in Tehran with thousands of chanting and flag-waving devotees around him. Just a few blocks down the streets, protesters chanted back and some were running away from the police, trying to avoid being smashed by their riot clubs.

Ahmadinejad's supporters commented on how he was the only candidate that cared about the common people of Iran and will defend them against the policies of any foreign powers or any negative faction inside Iran.

KHAMENEI BREAKS SILENCE

T his was by far the largest street protest and demonstration in the history of Iran since the 1979 Iranian Revolution. The hundreds of thousands of upset supporters of the defeated reform candidate Mir Hussein Mousavi marched the streets of Tehran and other cities, defying the official protest ban. Mousavi appeared for the first time in public at a rally staged by his supporters in Tehran after the landslide election win of Ahmadinejad, in the hope of calming the now-growing demonstrations.

What some hoped to be a calm protest turned out to be a riotous one as the protesters vented out their frustration and dismay about their candidate's loss in the June 12th election. In order to quell the protests, the Iranian security forces and the uncompromising militia continued to act with force and arrest the protesters, causing them to revolt further. The revolution only led to the supporters' incurring of injuries from the beatings of the government's militia. Brothers' blood was shed on the streets of Tehran as the rioters fought back and the militia fired guns from rooftops.

Iran's supreme leader and most powerful figure, Ayatollah Ali Khamenei, drew a hard line that posed as a ploy for Iran's opposition protesters to either halt any further protests over the June 12th disputed election or risk a violent crackdown. Ayatollah Ali Khamenei issued this warning during his stern sermon in Tehran. He warned the protesters and opposition leaders that they would be held personally responsible if the street protests did not end.

Uncompromisingly, Khamenei told the protesters to drop their demands for a new election and insisted that last week's presidential votes had been transparent. He said that the Islamic Republic does not alter vote counts as the system does not allow cheating. At the end of the sermon, Khamenei added that if the protesters will not obey and still pursue protesting, he will unleash the military force. Khamenei's warning seemed to not have any effect because shortly after dusk, cries of "Allahu Akbar" and "Death to the dictator" were shouted from the rooftops as the protesters began their first sign of resistance.

DEATH OF NEDA

One particular demonstration in Tehran on June 20, 2009, instantly caught the media's attention around the world because of a video captured by a bystander's mobile phone. This video captured graphic footage of a young woman being shot in the chest by what has been said to be Basij snipers. Neda Soltan, a young Iranian woman 26 years of age, was present at the demonstration just by chance. She hadn't been on the scene of the demonstration long when she was suddenly shot in her chest. Neda was rushed to the hospital but, tragically, had died before they even arrived. Even if a doctor had been present at the scene, he could not have prevented her death.

The footage that was shot from the mobile phone was instantly uploaded to YouTube, the popular site for sharing videos. This was not the first video footage of the Iranian demonstrations that was posted on YouTube, but it was the first time the world saw such a graphic murder of an innocent young woman. This video alone fueled the "Green

Movement" with a newfound cause—Neda. It allowed people around the world to see what was actually happening in the streets of Iran. Neda's story has become the most powerful one of the "Green Movement" yet.

The only reason Neda was in the streets was because of a traffic jam caused by the commotion. She and her music teacher left a car stuck in traffic to escape the heat. She was merely walking down the street talking on her phone when she was shot. She was a philosophy student and part-time travel agent and was not a protestor, although she was sympathetic toward the demonstrators.

Some say she may have been targeted because she was using a cell phone. Interestingly enough, the name "Neda" means "call" or "voice." Authorities did not want to release her body and agreed to only if her family would give her a quick burial on the outskirts of Tehran. A memorial service was planned but was canceled when the government would not allow it to proceed. The government even warned all mosques in the area against holding a memorial service for her. It is tradition for martyrs to have mourning ceremonies to be held on the third, seventh, and fortieth day after they have died, however these ceremonies were not permitted by the Iranian regime.

Iranian youth display the V for "Victory" sign.
Photography by Hamed Saber.

Iranian soldiers join the crowd of demonstrators.
Photography by Hamed Saber.

Iranian man displaying picture of riot police
beating protestors. Photography by Hamed Saber.

By Hamed Saber

A female Mousavi supporter flashes the V for "Victory." Photography by Hamed Saber.

Iranian displays the popular statement "Where is my vote?" Photography by Hamed Saber.

By Hamed Saber

Eid of Mab'as
Mousavi had a meeting with families of arrested
people. Photography by Hamed Saber.

Demonstrations at Azadi Square, Iran.
Photography by Hamed Saber.

Pro-Mousavi demonstrators show signs of support.
Photography by Hamed Saber.

By Hamed Saber - http://flickr.com/hamed

Women played an active role in the demonstrations. Photography by Hamed Saber.

Iranian flashes V for "Victory." Photography by
Hamed Saber.

CHAPTER 15 ۱۵

REPRESSION GROWS

At 7:30 a.m. in Tehran, the coercion of the "security forces" against the opposition had already escalated to a point that was considered to be the most aggressive since the presidential election. Iranian citizens woke up to scenes in the street only fit for a movie. A city bus had been set on fire during the night and the smoldering wreckage only further illustrated the devastation that this country was experiencing. What seemed to be chaos at this point, however, was only a small glimpse of the near future for the Iranian people. The citizens of Iran should brace themselves for the likelihood of more bloody altercations between the security forces and protesters on the streets of Tehran and elsewhere.

At 10:25 a.m., the Iranian state television reported that 10 people were killed as the police and protesters clashed in the streets of Tehran in lieu of the protesters' defiance to Ayatollah Ali Khamenei. Reports said there were at least another 100 protesters severely injured during the clashes.

Mousavi and his supporters received more official threats, one, of which, was in the form of a letter which said:

> It is your duty not to incite and invite the public to illegal gatherings; otherwise, you will be responsible for its consequences. It is your responsibility to prevent the public from attending such rallies instead of making accusations against the law enforcement.
>
> We believe this is an organized network which is most probably affiliated with foreign-related groups and deliberately disturbs the peace and security of the public. Of course, we have already ordered the law enforcement forces to deal with the issue.

Mousavi, in response to the threats, appeared at a demonstration in southern Tehran and called for a sit-in if he were to be arrested. He proudly announced to his supporters that he is ready to be a martyr. He is still firm on his call for nullifying the results of the election as the opposition supporters continue on insisting that the election was fraught with foul play.

Even U.S. President Obama called the government of Iran's reaction as "Violent and unjust." Previously, President Obama expressed "deep concerns" over the election. He vowed to stay out of the situation, yet was concerned about the hostility and asked that the rights of peaceful protesters be recognized. He added that he and the world have concerns about the validity of the election.

President Obama expressed worry when violence was directed at peaceful protestors and at their suppression. However, many express dismay that he did not show enough support for the Iranian people. Nevertheless, he said he hoped the Iranian people would take the correct steps to express themselves and said he would still pursue diplomacy with the government of Iran on its nuclear program and other subjects.

On June 21st at 7:30 a.m. in Tehran, confrontation broke out between some self-proclaimed "security forces" (Basij militia) and a large group of the opposition. It took no time to escalate to a point that was considered to be the most aggressive force used by the Basij since the presidential election.

A city bus had been set on fire in the night, and the smoldering wreckage only further illustrated the devastation that this country was experiencing. This type of destruction was commonly done by people trying to create a wall of smoke, in hopes that they could run to safety. We know from tweets coming from the front lines that burning tires let off the thickest, darkest clouds of smoke.

It didn't look like much was being done to stop the demonstrations this particular day. Grand Ayatollah Hossein Ali Montazeri called for 3 days of national mourning for those who were killed in protests and for the release of detained protesters.

Ahmadinejad reprimanded the United States and United Kingdom for making comments when they had no right to do so. He suggested they rectify their meddling positions. UK Foreign Minister David Millibrand denied the implication that protesters in Iran were motivated by other countries.

OFFICIALS BLAME THE WEST

Government officials in Iran have made it clear that they believe that the Western media and the governments of the United States as well as the United Kingdom have played a large part in the postelection violence and turmoil.

It was reported that Mousavi condemned the arrests of his supporters. That wasn't the only thing going on in Iran. News reporters from all over the world were being expelled from the country. Journalists from BBC were ejected from the country. Al Arabiya TV's Tehran office had been closed on the 12th, being cited by Iranian authorities for unfair reporting of the election. They were ordered to stay shut down. Journalists from *Newsweek* were detained without charge. About 23 local journalists and bloggers were detained.

Supporters of the opposition were urged by Mir Hussein Mousavi to rally in Haft-e Tir Square, Tehran, and despite stern warnings of a crackdown by the Revolutionary Guards, thousands of pro-reform supporters took to the streets to show their support for the martyrs that had lost their lives since the election.

In an answer to the call made by Mousavi, Ali Shahrokhi, head of the Iranian judiciary committee, stated that the Iranian government would pursue legal action against the defeated presidential candidate.

Ali Akbar Hashemi Rafsanjani, influential politician, former president, chairman of the Assembly of Experts, a body of the Mujtahids, and supporter of Mousavi, had not been seen or heard from since the election. It was feared he was being detained because of his beliefs. His daughter had been detained and released right after the election. Many believed that he was in the holy city of Qom, trying to put together a religious and political coalition that could take over the current government of President Ahmadinejad. There is some concern about what Rafsanjani was up to, and it seemed that he was more of a concern than the protesters in the streets.

INTERNAL DIVISIONS MOUNT

I ran's Press TV reported that the country's Interior Minister, Sadeq Mahsouli, was called to parliament to answer questions about his role and reaction to the protests since the election.

Mahsouli was asked to expand upon controversial issues, including the recent night raids on university dormitories and private residences. He took responsibility for failing to arrest the unknown group of people responsible for the attacks. Lawmakers reprimanded him for what they called "a lack of crisis management during the nine consecutive days of nationwide turmoil."

Iranian Parliament Speaker Ali Larijani expressed his deepest concern over the Interior Ministry's course of action towards the postvote developments. Larijani, in a rare internal criticism, held the Interior Ministry responsible for the recent attacks against citizens and university students.

"The Interior Ministry should clarify why the security forces destroyed the building and why students were injured or even killed," said Larijani. The Majlis speaker also recommended fresh television debates, asserting that "the voice of the people who have taken to the streets in millions should be heard."

—Iran's Press TV

Kayhan, the newspaper affiliated with the supreme leader, printed an article that explained how Mousavi would be arrested. Also, President Obama stated that he strongly condemned the actions of the Iranian government's beating of protestors and their imprisonment from the last few days. He also praised the Iranian people for their courage.

The BBC reported that guards broke into Mousavi's newspaper and Web site and arrested the entire staff. Other incidents include six members of the Iranian team playing in the World Cup that wore green wristbands during the competition to support Mousavi. Once they returned to Iran, the whereabouts of the players sporting the wristbands were unknown, and the others did not have their passports returned to them.

JUNE 24, 2009

The International Campaign for Human Rights in Iran released numbers today of those that have been arrested or killed since the election of June 12, 2009. The list shows 240 people that have been detained, which include 29 people that have already been released. The list further shows that of those 240, 102 are political figures, 23 journalists, 79 university students, and 7 university faculty members. The statement also states that the Iranian government has admitted to 27 casualties as a result of the protests, although many of the people on the streets of Iran, as well as members of the campaign, believe this to be a gross understatement of the bloodshed that has occurred.

Reports surface today that Neda Agha-Soltan was murdered for the purpose of propaganda by either anti-regime militants or the BBC. Both groups have staunchly denied any part in her death.

Apparently the family of Soltan was ordered out of their home by the Iranian authorities. Neighbors reported hearing her mother and father screaming in grief, and neighbors went out into the street to protest her death. The police descended on the family as soon as they found out a friend of the dead girl had come to visit the family at their flat. It is tradition for a family to attach a mourning announcement on a black banner to the home, and the family had done this. The police quickly pulled the banner down and insisted the family show no signs of mourning. Then the family was forced to move out.

Neighbors were warned not to say anything about her death. Neighbors report that the secret police patrolled the streets around the home. Many people tried to show their respects to the family but were turned away, and some were too afraid to do anything. When someone dies in Iran, the family isn't left to themselves for weeks, but this family will have to endure their loss alone. Neda Soltan was looked upon as a kind, innocent girl that everyone in the neighborhood respected.

JUNE 25, 2009

After not being seen in public in a week, Mir Hussein Mousavi reports on his newspaper's Web site that *"I am pressured to abandon my demand for the vote annulment ... a major rigging has happened ... I am prepared to prove that those behind the rigging are responsible for the bloodshed ... Continuation of legal and calm protests will guarantee achieving our goals."*

—Reuters, June 25, 2009

According to John Simpson of the BBC, he has come across members of the military in recent days that have had a change of heart since the election and are now supporters of Mousavi. They believe, like Mousavi, that the elections were indeed rigged.

Ahmadinejad suggested that President Obama express regret over the intrusion into Iranian politics brought on by the election, but President Obama denied any interference.

In Italy, a meeting of foreign ministers from eight countries took place. The mission of this meeting was to knit together a mutual standing on what had been happening in Iran. The Italians wanted Iran to know they did not approve of the actions that have happened since the election, yet they wanted to emphasize that they did not want to isolate Iran. They hoped to bring about a conversation with the involved parties in Iran and denounced the use of extreme violence.

A French company that distributes caviar to Iran boycotted the country. The owner said he will not supply a country that treats its people the way they do.

The doctor that came to the side of Neda Soltan wanted to tell her story so that her death wouldn't have been in vain. He is a student in England and said he realizes he may never be able to return to his home country of Iran after he publicizes the incident.

A Web site called NedaNet was developed for those who want to help Iranian citizens. They set up proxy servers that will help them publicize what is going on in the country. Iran is censoring many different media and is trying to stop news from getting out about what is truly happening in the country. This site will aid in the quest to let the world understand what the Iranian citizens have to deal with. The site warns Iranians that everything they do could be monitored and the punishment could include death.

JUNE 26, 2009

After hours of service interruption that opposition leaders are calling a massive attack on the rights of the people of Iran to voice their opinions to the world, the twitters rapidly pour in from the front lines of the protest. Even SMS service was temporarily unavailable, but was only out for a few minutes, stirring frenzy among opposition supporters.

Further reports from Reuters state that protests have slacked off during the day, but have not gone away. Peaceful protestors in the streets of Tehran told BBC News sources that they will continue their fight to elect the man into office that is the people's obvious choice.

Mousavi's supporters in the streets loudly proclaim that numbers of this size multitude would have surely put their candidate into office.

Green balloons were released clandestinely in the skies of Tehran in the afternoon in silent protest concerning the election and all the death and destruction it has created. The Iranian embassy in Sweden was attacked with firebombs and about 150 protesters tried to gain entrance. There was no news that they actually got inside.

There were reports that Saeed Mortazavi, prosecutor-general of Iran, was directed to take charge of the interrogation of detained demonstrators and journalists. Human rights groups are up in arms as this is the man who has been implicated in the death of a Canadian photojournalist in 2003. Mortazavi has the nickname of "butcher of the press" because he has shut down more than 100 newspapers and blogs that he thought went against the regime.

JUNE 27, 2009

The Guardian Council spoke to Press TV and said that the investigations into the election on the 12th that had been going on the past 10 days found no major irregularities. They did not find any indications of fraud. They also stated that they would convene a committee that would recount the votes. This committee would include representatives from all four candidates.

JUNE 28, 2009

Akbar Hashemi Rafsanjani finally spoke out in public. He stated that the events after the election were put into place as a conspiracy to divide the people of Iran and the Islamic system. He also praised the decision to extend the amount of time objections raised concerning the election could be looked into.

Bon Jovi and Andy Madadian, popular Iranian American musicians, recorded a new version of "Stand by Me." They did this to support the people of Iran and send them a message of global solidarity.

JUNE 29, 2009

The Guardian Council upheld the results of the June 12th election. Police flooded the streets in

Tehran and were inspecting IDs and checking cars in anticipation of any protests or violence.

There were many incidents. Automobiles on the parkway beeped their horns in protest, and the Basij smashed windshields and slashed tires. Some cell phone service was shutdown. There were plans to form a human chain from Tajrish Square to the railway, but police positioned themselves across Valiasr Street and Daneshju Park to stop it.

BBC Persian reported that Gholam Hossein Mohseni-Ejeie, minister of intelligence, came up with a new way of prosecuting individuals that had been detained or arrested. He divided them into three groups consisting of:

1. Individuals who were involved in decision making concerned with current events. They remained in custody until a decision was made concerning their actions

2. Demonstrators who took advantage of the situation. These individuals would not be freed. Plans for a new tribunal to be set up to deal with these people were in the process.

3. Those individuals that were under the influence of the events taking place. These people would be freed if they had not been already.

JUNE 30, 2009

Photos of ballots from the June 12th election were posted by Iran State Media. It was noted that most of them were in perfect condition, not folded or rolled, and everyone knows most people fold them before putting them in the ballot box. The photos also showed that many of the ballots had the same pen and handwriting, as if a single person wrote them all.

A student that had been taken in custody told his story via Twitter. He said he was in a room with 200 other people and there was no room to sit, there was also one toilet they all had to share, which was impossible. He said they were handcuffed for a day and a half and detainees were hit periodically although rarely in the face. During the second day, people came in with confessions all prewritten in different handwriting and forced the detainees to sign them. These papers all stated that they were members of a pro-Mousavi organization.

BASIJ ON THE OFFENSIVE

"But the Iran of today is not the Iran of three weeks ago; it is in volatile flux from without and within. Its Robespierres are running amok. Obama must do nothing to suggest business as usual. Let Ahmadinejad, he of the bipolar mood swings, fret and sweat. Let him writhe in the turbid puddle of his self-proclaimed "justice" and "ethics."

—Roger Cohen from *The New York Times,* July 1, 2009

The Basij militia is targeting Mousavi and his wife, Zahra Rahnavard, and accusing them of nine counts against the state that could result in 10 years in prison.

The doctor who went to the aid of fallen student Neda Soltan has been interviewed by several countries since he left Iran. The Iranian Intelligence Ministry stated that they were looking for him.

Press TV reported that the Iranian ministry warned that "Any activities by the election headquarters in provinces, cities, and districts will no longer have a legal basis."

JULY 2, 2009

The people of Iran are begging for international support to continue. One anonymous Iranian student posted this comment on Facebook: "Make no mistake about it; the revolution in Iran has passed a tipping point and entered into a new phase. In this period, the worst thing that the Western media can do is to allow itself to get distracted." It is not coincidence that the day this comment was posted was the same day that news had reached Iran that pop superstar Michael Jackson had died.

JULY 3, 2009

The G8 Summit is planning to discuss financial sanctions against Iran in response to the activities there since the June 12th election. It was reported that the United States is opposed to these sanctions.

Saeed Hajarian, a reformist theorist who was attacked by an assassin in March of 2000 and became severely disabled because of this attack, was detained after the Iranian election. It was reported that he was in extreme discomfort because of his disability. Interrogators were unable to get him to talk, but it was said that the man couldn't talk because of the pain he experiencing.

Interrogators continually pushed down on his bad shoulder and kept asking him what he was trying to do as a member of the Green Revolution. The man had a hard time talking in the first place because of his injuries, and his interrogators were only making it worse. Tehran Broadcast published a plea for his release.

JULY 4, 2009

The Association of Researchers and Teachers of Qum, a city in Iran, called the new Iranian government illegitimate.

JULY 5, 2009

A directive came to the Iranian courts that those individuals who work with satellite TV or Internet Web sites can get a prison sentence up to 10 years. Since the election on June 12th, satellite TV and Web sites have been shut down or censored. More than 1,000 people were arrested.

Mousavi planned for a new political party. The platform would be to control the power of the leadership in the republic. He is expected to file paperwork prior to the beginning of Ahmadinejad's next 4-year term.

Ahmadinejad was reported to desire to speak with President Obama in front of international media at the United Nations. He called it "diplomatic activity." Previously, he voiced a desire to debate Obama before an audience of the UN. This new request seemed very similar.

JULY 6, 2009

Not much had been heard from Rafsanjani's party since the election, but on July 6th, he gave the approval for the party to reject the results of the election. The party gave several demands, including a return of public confidence after the final vote count, analysis of violence against protesters, release of political prisoners, and the censorship and shutting down of the media to stop.

Two doctors in Iran at the time of the protests published a story in the French newspaper *La Figaro*. These doctors fled to France before giving an account of events in Tehran. Hospitals in the area had about 92 deaths attributed to conflicts with militia and Iranian police. The official toll in Iran was published at 17. They reported that a woman who was 8 months pregnant was included in this number, as were six young males whose bodies were found on the outskirts of Shahriar. These men had wounds in the neck, but their skulls had been smashed and brains removed in order to retrieve bullets and hide evidence.

Interestingly, the Pollution Committee of Tehran has decided to close government agencies, factories, and schools for 2 days because of "heavy pollution." This period of time is the same as the 10-year anniversary of the 18 Tir student protests. A national strike was expected that day, and this would circumvent the activity.

JULY 7 & 8, 2009

President Ahmadinejad appeared in a broadcast and criticized foreign meddling following the presidential election. He accused other countries of contributing to the unrest after the election. He also noted that his opponents had called the election rigged without any supporting evidence.

Tehran University stated that authorities closed down the dorms for 2 weeks. Normally, during the anniversary of the 1999 student uprisings, the dorms are closed for a few days to prevent demonstrations and other events. This year, the time has been extended to 2 weeks.

ANNIVERSARY OF THE 1999 UPRISINGS

I t was the 10th anniversary of the 1999 student uprisings at Tehran University.

The atmosphere of demonstrations in the streets seems to have a different tone than those in the past days. Marches aren't occurring as frequently, but groups of 200 to 300 individuals continued to gather. They refused to move when attacked by the police. The Basij's continue to prevent large groups from gathering, but the demonstrators are making sure they stay in smaller groups.

There didn't seem to be any shootings, but there was tear gas. These demonstrations are not in support of Mousavi; instead, they are an indication to the regime that the people of Iran will not keep their silence.

As a note: At least 35 Iranian journalists have been arrested since protests against the results of recent elections began. Some foreign journalists were also detained. Iason Athanasiadis, a Greek-British reporter, was held for 3 weeks in Tehran's Evin Prison. He's now back home in Athens.

Thousands of protesters streamed down avenues of the capital Thursday, chanting "Death to the dictator" and defying security forces that fired tear gas and charged with batons, witnesses said. The first opposition foray into the streets in 11 days aimed to revive mass demonstrations that were crushed in Iran's postelection turmoil.

Iranian authorities had promised tough action to prevent the marches, which supporters of opposition leader Mir-Hossein Mousavi have been planning for days in Internet messages. Heavy police forces deployed at key points in the city ahead of the marches, and Tehran's governor vowed to "smash" anyone who heeded the demonstration calls.

In some places, police struck hard. Security forces chased after protesters, beating them with clubs on Valiasr Street, Tehran's biggest north-south avenue, witnesses said.

Women in headscarves and young men dashed away, rubbing their eyes as police fired tear gas in footage aired on state-run Press TV. In a photo from Thursday's events in Tehran obtained by The Associated Press outside Iran, a woman with her black headscarf looped over her face raised a fist in front of a garbage bin that had been set on fire.

But the clampdown was not absolute. At Tehran University, a line of police blocked a crowd from reaching the gates of the campus, but then did not move to disperse them as the protesters chanted, "Mir Hossein" and "Death to the dictator" and waved their hands in the air, witnesses said. The crowd grew to nearly 1,000 people, the witnesses reported.

"Police, protect us," some of the demonstrators chanted, asking the forces not to move against them, stated The Associated Press.

The protesters appeared to reach several thousand, but their full numbers were difficult to determine since marches took place in several parts of the city simultaneously and protesters mingled with passersby. There was no immediate word on arrests or injuries.

It did not compare to the hundreds of thousands who joined the marches that erupted after the June 12 presidential election, protesting what the opposition said were fraudulent results. But it was a show of determination despite a crackdown that has cowed protesters for nearly 2 weeks.

Onlookers and pedestrians often gave their support. In side streets near the university, police were chasing young activists, and when they caught one, passersby chanted, "Let him go, let him go," until the policemen released him. Elsewhere, residents let fleeing demonstrators slip into their homes to elude police, witnesses said.

All witnesses spoke on condition of anonymity for fear of government reprisals. Iranian authorities have imposed restrictions that ban reporters from leaving their offices to cover demonstrations.

Many of the marchers were young men and women, some wearing green surgical masks, the color of Mousavi's movement, but older people joined them in some places. Vehicles caught in traffic honked their horns in support of the marchers, witnesses said. Police were seen with a pile of license plates, apparently pried off honking cars in order to investigate the drivers later, witnesses reported.

CHAPTER 20 ٢٠

CALM BEFORE THE STORM

Today, everything seems to be very calm and peaceful in the sense that there has been no such great event pertaining towards any conflict with governmental forces for at least a week; however, there is a relatively large movement slowly and gradually taking place behind the scene. It has also been affirmed that Ex-President Ayatollah Rafsanjani is taking over the Friday prayers offered in Tehran University once again. Unconfirmed is if Mousavi and Khatami will also attend these prayers as well. It is still unknown whether or not this is a trap for the protesters and what Rafsanjani has to say about it.

Another thing that is still unconfirmed is if Rafsanjani will team up with the government, Mousavi, or plead for a consolidation and be an unpleasant opposition. It is also said that the government could possibly treat its people in an "unpleasant manner." The effect of this movement, however, could be a support for the people or would drive them into an Iranian Civil War.

Due to this uncertainness, the Friday prayers shall be listened to carefully as this might be one of the greatest turnabouts during the movement. No matter what Rafsanjani does, it is not a given that people will believe in his actions and start to follow him, as it just might not be in accordance with what the people want. As the Iranian population had completely formed the 18 Tir, due to this, no one from Mousavi's group was related to any of the protests. There are articles in newspapers, like the *LA Times* or *Tehran Bureau,* which prove a study on Mousavi and Khatami being left behind in this movement.

One of the most interesting things about this movement is that Ahmadinejad will be in Mashhad, the holiest city, whereas just a few weeks ago, he was not permitted to travel there and instead, had to stay back in Tehran because there was no guarantee of his safety and security!

After a long absence, Hashemi Rafsanjani shall be leading the Friday prayers as he is a very strong entity of the Iranian establishment and an ardent supporter of Mir-Hossein Mousavi opposing Ahmadinejad right before the elections. State media, IRNA, Raja, and Iran newspapers are picturing this event with no importance at all and are building up controversies for his removal.

Rafsanjani is one of the major key players of the powerful Assembly of Experts, which is officially assigned as an administration in appointing the supreme leader. He is accused of violating various laws by which he can be discharged from at least one of his roles in the government. Article 141 of Iran's Constitution being applicable to the Expediency Council has been published by IRNA and Raja, Iran newspapers. Article 141 prohibits governmental employees from holding more than one position. As Rafsanjani is leading the Expediency Council, Article 141 does not apply in his case.

JULY 17, 2009

The man with a loudspeaker screams: "Death to U.S., death to Israel, death to the infidels, death to England," and so on, but the crowd answers, "Death to Russia" EVERY time.

JULY 20, 2009

In what may be another sign that Iran's authorities are trying to disrupt opposition protests online, a blogger using the screen name "mms7778" has taken to posting this update every minute on Twitter:

#iranelection Ahmadinejad the president. Man with clear judgment. Will be inaugurated soon again. The same blogger posts obscene insults attacking Iran's opposition supporters in between each repetition of his praise for Mr. Ahmadinejad. By using the tag "#iranelection" in each update, this anonymous blogger ensures that people searching Twitter for news of the protests will continuously encounter these insults.

Suspicion that Iran's blogging community has been infiltrated by double agents has sown fears and doubt online. For instance, a few days ago, Omid Habibinia, an Iranian now blogging from Switzerland, wrote on Twitter about a rumor that a significant figure in Iran's blogging community is a double agent: *"Some bloggers [are] saying Hossein Derakhshan (missing since 8 month ago) is working with intelligence agents."**

Mr. Derakhshan is an Iranian-Canadian who played a large role in getting Iran's blogging movement going in the first place. Mr. Derakhshan mysteriously disappeared after his return to Iran from Canada in 2008. The fact that his stance had seemed to soften on Iran's government had dismayed several of his fellow bloggers before he went missing. In 2006, he had made a point of challenging government dogma by traveling to Israel and blogging about it.

His name was briefly mentioned in Iranian news reports in connection with the case of Roxana Saberi, the Iranian-American journalist convicted on espionage charges.

When Iranian President Mahmoud Ahmadinejad sent a letter to Tehran's chief prosecutor, asking that Ms. Saberi, who was charged with spying for the United States, be given an opportunity to present a full defense, he also requested the same treatment for Hossein Derakhshan, the Iranian-Canadian blogger who was arrested last November and charged with spying for Israel.

After we published that previous blog post on Mr. Derakhshan, one of our readers, Javad Ghorbati, commented:

"It also should be stated that many Internet-based Iranian communities are skeptical and puzzled about Hossein Derakhshan's (aka Hoder) work and his relationship with the Iranian authorities." There is a silent agreement within them that Mr. Derakhshan may have been employed by the Iranian authorities to collect information on Internet-based

Iranian activists during recent years when he was heavily involved with developing the Iranian blogosphere. As it is widely reported, the Iranian Revolutionary Guard, which is known as the core of the Iranian intelligent service, has been recently involved with creating a new division for surveillance of the political Web sites and weblogs on the religious and national security grounds, and many Iranian believes that Hossein Derakhshan might have some involvement with the new division.

While there is no evidence to support the rumor that Mr. Derakhshan is cooperating with the authorities in their battle against Iran's opposition bloggers—and the people running the online campaign to free Mr. Derakhshan vehemently deny the rumor—the fact that some Iranian bloggers are again talking about this possibility seems to indicate that the "cyber army" set up by Iran's Revolutionary Guards has helped to stir up paranoia and fear in that community.

Last month, a series of updates were posted on Twitter by a blogger who identified himself as a member of the Revolutionary Guard who seemed to be dedicated to finding and helping to arrest opposition protesters and bloggers. Even if Mr. Derakhshan has not defected to the side of Iran's security forces, it is clear that some Internet-savvy people have taken the fight to suppress the opposition's protests online.

The Iranian blogger, Omid Habibinia, working from Switzerland, says that this video, uploaded to YouTube on Tuesday, shows members of the Basij militia on Tehran's streets today, near Haft-e Tir Square:

"If anyone familiar with Tehran can tell us if this looks like the part of the city where today's protests reportedly took place, we would appreciate hearing from you. Also, if anyone has seen this video uploaded before today, please let us know."

Karim Sadjadpour, an Iranian-American analyst at the Washington-based Carnegie Endowment for International Peace, told Reuters that "The main problem the opposition faces is that their brain trust is either in prison, under house arrest, or unable to communicate freely." Mr. Sadjadpour added, "There remains tremendous popular outrage, but at the moment, there is no leadership to channel that outrage politically."

Mr. Sadjadpour also pointed out that the country's ruling cleric, Ayatollah Ali Khamenei, effectively governs now thanks to the support of the country's security forces. "While there are pronounced cleavages among Iran's clerical elite,

Khamenei's power base is not the clergy but the Revolutionary Guards. When and if we start to see rifts among the Guards, it could be fatal for both Khamenei and Ahmadinejad."

JULY 22, 2009

This announcement was made by two Iranian intellectuals in support of Iranian protest in front of the United Nation:

"Today, you, the brave men and women at the doorstep of the United Nations hungrily and thirstily are telling the story of a nation that more than any place or any time is hungry for freedom and thirsty for justice; and just like the United Nations that is located in New York, U.S., but does not only belong to the New Yorkers or Americans but to the entire human race, today, the 'Green Movement' of Iran does not only belong to Mousavi or religious people or reformists, but to all Iranians."

CHAPTER 21   ٢١

FIRST DEPUTY RESIGNATION

Ahmadinejad's first deputy, Rahim Mashaei, resigned. The supreme leader ordered him to do so 6 days prior, but Ahmadinejad resisted the order. After the supreme leader's order, Mashaei said he didn't consider himself first deputy and he would serve the Revolution and Iran.

The U.S. Senate passed an unanimous vote to adopt legislation that will allow the Iranian people to get access to media information regardless of the electronic censorship they are receiving from their current government. It gave $30 million to Broadcasting Board of Governors to develop broadcasting into Iran through Radio Free Europe. This money can be used to create technology to counter the blocks the Iranian government set up. It also authorized $20 million to develop an "Iranian Electronic Education, Exchange, and Media Fund," supporting Web sites that will allow the Iranian people to share information. This legislation requires a report on non-Iranian companies that have helped the Iranian government censorship efforts. It authorizes another $5 million for the U.S. secretary of state to monitor information concerning human rights that have occurred since the June 12th election.

JULY 25, 2009

July 25, 2009, is the designated day of Global Day of Action, which was coordinated by human-rights organizations. It was an effort to demand human rights for the Iranian people and show solidarity with the civil rights movement in Iran.

JULY 29, 2009

Reports from Tehran families in recent days who have received the bodies of relatives arrested at opposition rallies and who later died from violent treatment in prison have fueled anger at the government.

Among the dead is Mohsen Rouhalamini, the son of a prominent conservative and adviser to presidential candidate Mohsen Rezai. His family said he died of cardiac arrest and bleeding in his lungs, and that his face had been smashed.

News of his death in prison last week spurred fury across political lines, prompting even some pro-government newspapers and lawmakers to charge the regime with excessive use of force and violence in crushing its opposition. Opposition leaders warned of a backlash and urged the government of President Mahmoud Ahmadinejad to reverse its actions.

"People will not forgive these acts. How could it be possible that someone goes into a prison, then his body comes out?" opposition leader Mir-Hossein Mousavi said Monday in a meeting with teachers.

Some of the families say they are speaking out despite being warned against speaking to the media and holding funerals and memorial services. On receiving the bodies, they say, they were told to sign consent forms that named the cause of death as meningitis, flu, or bacterial infection.

In addition, scores of protesters who have been detained and released in the past few weeks are now coming forth with details of their arrest and prison conditions. These accounts paint a disturbing picture of widespread abuse and torture by interrogators in detention facilities that are overflowing.

The opposition has called for a nationwide protest on Thursday to commemorate the deaths of Neda Agha-Soltan and others killed in violent protests on June 20, because in Shiite Islam, it is the custom to hold a memorial service on the 40th day after a person's death.

Iran's regime appears to be responding to the pressures, seemingly wary of an even deeper divide in an already-volatile political landscape. On Tuesday, it released 140 detained protesters, and Supreme Leader Ayatollah Ali Khamenei ordered the closure of a detention facility in south Tehran known as Kahrizak where protesters were being held. Before this, it had been used to jail drug dealers.

The parliament last week named a special committee to investigate the conditions of prisoners and facilities after hundreds of families wrote to lawmakers complaining about lack of transparency and reports of abuse.

According to independent human-rights organizations, over 1,000 people have been arrested and nearly 100 killed after the June 12 presidential election upset. Among the arrested are 250 prominent reformers, journalists, lawyers, and student activists.

"The regime's first priority is survival. First, they repress violently and now they realize their legitimacy is badly tarnished, so they are trying to defuse the incredible anger by people," said Payam Akhavan, a former prosecutor at The Hague and cofounder of Iran Human Rights Documentation Center in New Haven, Conn.

Last week, families who had missing relatives were taken to a cold-storage facility normally used for fruits and vegetables in the south of Tehran that had been turned into a morgue. Pictures posted on Iranian Web sites showed bodies piled on top of one another as families tried to identify loved ones.

Among the bodies released recently to relatives in Tehran, Ramin Ghahremani, 30, died in the hospital because of internal bleeding in his chest. He was beaten and hung upside down for long periods, according to his mother, who spoke with him while he was in the hospital.

Amir Javadifard, 27, a graduate student in industrial management, had broken bones and bruises, according to his father, Ali Javadifard, who saw his son in the hospital before he died. On Monday, Mr. Javadifard was taken to a morgue and received his son's body.

"My son was healthy and well when they arrested him, and his body was returned to me in a different condition," Mr. Javadifard said.

JULY 30, 2009

Iranian police forced opposition leader Mir-Hossein Mousavi to leave a Tehran cemetery where hundreds of mourners had gathered to commemorate victims of the unrest that erupted after the June presidential election. "Police forced Mousavi to return to his car and leave the cemetery. Police are also warning mourners to leave the place or face the consequences," a witness told Reuters.

CHAPTER 22 ٢٢

AHMADINEJAD'S INAUGURATION

For the first time in weeks, the regime was on the offensive. Ayatollah Jannati's tough address at Friday prayers in Tehran was followed by the showpiece trial of almost 100 defendants, including a former vice president and deputy ministers, key members of reformist political parties, and journalists.

Regarding the legal process, the courtroom scene was, to be frank, ludicrous. There were no defense lawyers, and the only official press in the courtroom were those from media favorable to the state.

The indictment and presentation of charges offered no evidence of substantive criminal acts apart from the relatively minor acts of throwing stones at security forces. More sinister allegations of bombing relied upon the past, rather than the current, records of defendants and did not include any of the most prominent detainees. And the "foreign-plot" scenario was almost laughable. It turned U.S.-based academics into directors of an Iranian insurgency.

Abbas Milani is a solid historian and political analyst, and Gene Sharp works with theory, rather than application, of nonviolent regime change. Mark Palmer may be an irritating polemicist, but he is not a CIA mastermind.

The central act of the prosecution's play was the testimony of former Vice President Mohammad Ali Abtahi. While dramatic in its content, it offered no details of a treasonous plot. Instead, this was blatant political maneuver, designed to stigmatize Mohammad Khatami, Mehdi Karroubi, Mir-Hossein Mousavi (although he was portrayed as a naïve campaigner rather than malevolent schemer), and, above all, Hashemi Rafsanjani.

Only Abtahi knows whether his testimony was genuine or coerced. His family and attorney declared that he had been tortured and drugged. Pictures in the courtroom showed a man who looked haggard and unhealthy, someone who had lost a great deal of weight in detention. His "confession" had apparently been circulated in advance to news services, that would give it the "correct" interpretation.

Opposition politicians denounced both the trial and Abtahi's suspect testimony. Mousavi's camp declared, via *Ghalam News*, "The people's movement is peaceful in nature and relies on the demand of the public to achieve their rights which

have been trampled upon during the last elections."
They specifically ruled out the allegation of
conspiracy with foreign agents, responding not only
to the trial but some unhelpful calls from outside Iran
for regime change. "Despite claims of the dissidents,
this just and spiritual movement has no connections
with the foreigners and is completely domestic, and
our nation is mindful of staying away from
foreigners."

Rafsanjani was briefer in his response, calling
the testimony "an obvious lie." Significantly,
however, his advisors issued the statement through
the offices of the Expediency Council, which
Rafsanjani heads. The message to the regime: If you
want a fight, we have our own bases of support
within the system.

What matters in the short-term is not the cold
dissection of yesterday's events but the emotive
reaction. Will the regime succeed, days before the
anointing of Mahmoud Ahmadinejad as president, in
mobilizing public opinion against the opposition or
at least ensuring acceptance of its authority? Or is
this another instance of going too far in trying to
crush protest as illegitimate?

The challenge for the regime is that it cannot
sustain the high-profile denunciation on a daily
basis. It has played its strongest card with Abtahi.

Meanwhile, the opposition is countering. A show of dissent was scheduled for this morning outside the offices of the head of Iran's judiciary, and there is talk of protests not only for Wednesday, when Ahmadinejad is inaugurated, but also Monday, when he is approved by the supreme leader, and Friday, a day of celebration for Imam Mahdi's birthday.

It is one thing to crush a reformist faction like the Islamic Iran Participation Front, whose leading members are on trial. It is another to take on both the "Green Movement" and Rafsanjani by linking them so blatantly (and, I think, crudely).

The regime may "win" but, to do so, it is gambling. And far from cleaning up the resistance with an easy bet, it has to raise the stakes.

1440 GMT: Ali-Akbar Javanfekr, President Ahmadinejad's press secretary, has resigned from his post. Javanfekr stated that "there is a need for fresh blood to take over the responsibility, and one must make way for these individuals."

The Islamic Participation Front, one of the reformist parties, has responded to the trials via its news site Norouz:

"The show goes on: Wholesale killings and suppressions, wholesale arrests and wholesale trial and sentencing. The trial of the political activists arrested after the presidential elections has started. As it could have been expected and just as political activists and parties had warned, the trial was held eschewing all legal presuppositions favoring the defendants. The Islamic Participation Front states that the sole reporting news agency in the court was the pro-government and mendacious Fars news agency. Considering the track record of this agency in propagating falsehoods, it is obvious that none of the statements of this agency possess any credibility."

Norouz reports that a credible source located in the court has stated that none of the statements of Fars are true and the court is, effectively, a kangaroo court.

AUGUST 2, 2009

CORRESPONDENT MANI HAS PROVIDED AN ENGLISH TRANSLATION OF MIR-HOSSEIN MOUSAVI'S LATEST STATEMENT ON THE TEHRAN TRIALS AND THE MANOEUVRES OF THE REGIME:

It has been claimed that the children of the revolution have confessed in yesterday's court that they were colluding with foreign powers to overthrow the Islamic Republic. Personally, I have paid close attention [to these confessions] and I could not find anything to support this claim. On the contrary, [these so-called confessions] are painful statements of the painful conditions of the accused in the last fifty days.

When the spirit is crushed, individuals admit to everything their interrogators want, while, in fact, these confessions are just chronicles of woe.

These chronicles imply that Mohsen Roohul Amini [who died in detention] rightly chose to be a martyr; that if we [the prisoners] had not resisted for 50 days, this farce would have been performed earlier; that we [the prisoners] confessed to whatever they told us to so this would be obvious to all that these confessions were coerced out of us.

The teeth of the torturers and confessors has reached the bone, and now their policy is to find victims amongst individuals who have done great service to this country and this establishment and indeed have played the most sensitive roles in establishing it. Can you threaten those who yearned for martyrdom with anything less? Are you intending to target the foundation of Islam and the prestige of the establishment after slaughtering the basis of its republic? Observing such a kangaroo court leaves humanity no recourse but to indict those responsible for this trial of hitting a great low in morality and ethics and credibility.

These scenes that we observe are nothing other that a clumsy attempt [by a faction] to jump-start the [new] tenth government. They expect a court that is totally fraudulent to verify that no fraud has taken place. If you do not cheat, display your honesty by abiding with the basic procedures of a legal court process.

With such trivial indictments, by stating nonsense, by referring to three-penny publications, by basing your cases upon journalistic reports of dubious quality, and by invoking confessions that reek of the medieval justice system [of Europe], how do you expect to satisfy the people? Have you not read that the prophet [Mohammad] has stated that for a person that confesses after torture there can be no punishment, or that the prophet has stated that from a person that is imprisoned and consequently threatened no confession can be taken?

Our people sympathize with their children, whom they were only able to see after 50 days of uncertainty. Our dear [imprisoned] brothers, be not dejected! Be sure that the people understand your situation and know that your safety is of paramount importance. In the very near future the people will witness how those who performed these horrific iniquities will be legally prosecuted....As the holy book says ... the punishment of the oppressors will be visited upon them exactly at the time that God has determined.

AUGUST 3, 2009

The official event today will be the supreme leader's endorsement of President Ahmadinejad, who will be inaugurated on Wednesday, but this has already been eclipsed by other events. With Ahmadinejad a lame duck even before his second term starts, with the battle now between the regime and Hashemi Rafsanjani, as well as the regime and the Green opposition, and with the headline issue of detentions reinforced by the images of Saturday's trial, the focus will not be on Ayatollah Khamenei's formal declaration, but what he says in addition to it.

This will be the supreme leader's first significant public statement since his dispute with Ahmadinejad over the selection of the First Vice President Esfandiar Rahim-Mashai. Since then, the president has made an ambiguous statement about his position, both in general and specifically in relation to Khamenei. It is far from clear, however, that "conservative" and "principlist" blocs inside and outside Parliament—also angered by the firing of the Ministry of Intelligence and the attempted dismissal of three others—have reconciled with Ahmadinejad against the supposed threat of an opposition working with foreign elements and the real challenge of clerical and political criticism of the government's abuses of the legal system.

So, does Khamenei make any reference to either a new, resurgent beginning with the president or a lingering criticism of him? Or does he just let Ahmadinejad dangle by saying nothing of direct or implied substance?

Meanwhile, the opposition appears to be building its own reaction on Wednesday during Ahmadinejad's inauguration, rather than today. The talk now is of symbolic steps such as disruption of traffic, "flash" demonstrations, and power overloads, rather than any mass action. Indeed, it appears that the new impetus for the movement, again including Rafsanjani as well as other leaders and protestors, is the response to Saturday's trials. There is a very real and significant question of whether they can turn an initial defense (we are not guilty of a "plot") into a damaging assault on the government's credibility (they are guilty of degrading and abusing not only the detainees, but the revolution and Islam).

In that context, there are interesting signals from Press TV. While other state outlets, such as Fars News, were allowed to give full coverage from inside the courtroom, Press TV was shut out (probably because of confusion, rather than a deliberate action) along with opposition and foreign media. Pushed to the side on the direct reporting of the proceedings against the "enemy," Press TV has been giving airtime to blunt criticism of the regime, such as the challenge to the trial from reformist member of parliament and the reflections on prominent scientist/politician Abdolhossein Roohul Amini on his son Mohsen, who died in detention in Evin Prison.

AUGUST 4, 2009

Last week, even before he was officially endorsed as the winner of Iran's disputed June 12 presidential election, Mahmoud Ahmadinejad quietly assigned himself new powers by taking direct control of the country's intelligence ministry.

According to a report published on the English language Web site of Iran's parliament on Saturday, after Mr. Ahmadinejad fired the previous minister, Gholam-Hussein Mohseni-Ejei, he appointed himself "caretaker minister."

Even if he does not intend to hold on to the position, Mr. Ahmadinejad is in direct control of the Intelligence Ministry at a sensitive moment as the regime attempts to convict leading members of the opposition on charges with conspiring to overthrow the government on behalf of foreign powers.

The report notes that a conservative legislator called the move illegal:

The president's decision to act as the caretaker until a new cabinet is formed threw the country's polity into confusion.

Ahmad Tavakkoli, a senior Principlist representative from Tehran in the Majlis (Iran's parliament), accused the president of breaking the law. "By law, the caretaker of the Intelligence Ministry should have all the necessary requirements and qualifications of a '*Mujtahid*.'"

Islamic law defines *Mujtahid* as a male Islamic scholar who is competent enough to interpret divine law (Sharia) in practical situations using *Ijtihad* (independent thought). Tavakkoli criticized President Ahmadinejad for violating the constitution, saying he should have postponed the appointment of the intelligence minister until after the new cabinet is formed.

If his opponents in Iran's Parliament want to voice their displeasure at the move, they won't have to wait long. Mr. Ahmadinejad is scheduled to appear in parliament in a matter of hours to be sworn in for a second term as Iran's president on Wednesday morning in Tehran.

Outside the parliament building, according to a message posted on the Twitter feed Mousavi1388, which appears to be run by supporters of the opposition leader Mir Hussein Mousavi, a "peaceful protest" is planned. The message, posted on Tuesday, called for opposition supporters who claim that the presidential election was rigged to gather at 9 a.m. local time to protest as Mr. Ahmadinejad takes the oath of office inside the building.

AUGUST 5, 2009

The Associated Press reports that "Iran's main state TV channels did not offer live coverage of the ceremony in an apparent effort by the country's Islamic rulers to avoid emphasizing the boycotts to domestic audiences," but this video of the country's supreme leader handing a decree to Mr. Ahmadinejad was apparently included in a news report on a state channel.

Several reports have taken note of the awkward body language seen in the video between Ayatollah Khamenei and Mr. Ahmadinejad when there seemed to be some confusion about what sort of kiss would be exchanged.

The AP notes that 4 years ago, during the same ceremony, Mr. Ahmadinejad kissed Ayatollah Khamenei's hand "to show absolute loyalty," but this time, after some hesitation, Mr. Ahmadinejad kissed the supreme leader's shoulder instead. As The AP reports, this is "not a common gesture in Iran, where men often exchange kisses on the cheeks."

Some supporters of Iran's opposition suggested online that Mr. Ahmadinejad was trying to signal that he is not subservient to the country's ruling cleric, but Hooman Majd, an Iranian-American journalist and the author of *The Ayatollah Begs to Differ,* said that Mr. Ahmadinejad was criticized 4 years ago for kissing the leader's hand, which no previous president had done. Also, Mr. Majd says, "Kissing the shoulder is a sign of respect, certainly, to a cleric." Still, it is true that, as Matt Weaver points out on The Guardian's Web site, "the supreme leader did not embrace the president as he did 4 years ago."

According to the BBC, Iran's official IRNA news agency, later it was reported that Mr. Ahmadinejad had not kissed Ayatollah Khamenei's hand or cheek because he had a cold."

This report from Britain's ITN includes video of the same point in the same ceremony from 4 years ago and shows that two of Iran's former presidents,

Mohammad Khatami and Ali Akbar Hashemi Rafsanjani, who were absent today, were prominent figures last time, near center stage when Ayatollah Khamenei embraced Mr. Ahmadinejad.

Iran's state-supported English language broadcaster, Press TV, said that the ceremony was affected by the absence of former President Khatami, since "the endorsement decrees are normally read by the previous president—even for the second term of the new president in office." Press TV added that both of the opposition candidates who continue to contest the results of the June 12 election, Mir Hussein Mousavi and Mehdi Karroubi, also missed the ceremony. In 2005, the defeated candidate, former President Rafsanjani, was, of course, present.

Reuters reports that White House spokesman Robert Gibbs has retracted the statement he made on Tuesday, when he called Mahmoud Ahmadinejad "the elected leader" of Iran.

White House spokesman Robert Gibbs on Wednesday said he had misspoken in calling Mahmoud Ahmadinejad Iran's elected leader, and that Washington will let the Iranian people decide whether Iran's election was fair.

"Let me correct a little bit of what I said yesterday. I denoted that Mr. Ahmadinejad was the elected leader of Iran. I would say that's not for me to pass judgment on," Gibbs told reporters aboard Air Force One. "He's been inaugurated. That's a fact. Whether any election was fair, obviously, the Iranian people still have questions about that, and we'll let them decide about that."

According to a post on the National Iranian-American Council's blog, a White House official had said earlier that Mr. Gibbs, the president's spokesman, did not mean to say that Mahmoud Ahmadinejad had won the June 12 presidential election, but was referring to the 2005 election. NIAC reports:

"A major controversy erupted yesterday when White House press secretary Robert Gibbs said Ahmadinejad is Iran's "elected leader." NIAC has been told by a White House official that Gibbs was not recognizing Ahmadinejad as the winner of the most recent election, but was referring to the previous election."

For an administration that has taken pains not to take sides in Iran's election dispute, this obviously wasn't one of Gibbs' best moments. The statement was quickly picked up by Iran's state media.

In the absence of confirmation by other White House officials, this should be interpreted as a poorly constructed statement—and hopefully not the administration's policy. The administration has been walking a tightrope, condemning the human rights abuses in Iran while allowing Iranians to sort out their own election dispute.

President Obama himself has been the main driver behind the American approach to Iran, and he will have the final word, and one would hope that would involve more credible statements and policies.

AUGUST 6, 2009

Reporting from Tehran and Beirut—Dogged by allegations of election fraud and battered by some within his own conservative camp, Mahmoud Ahmadinejad limped defiantly into his second term as Iran's president Wednesday, vowing to strive for "national greatness."

As he was sworn in, the empty seats of reformist and moderate politicians boycotting the ceremony gaped from the gallery inside the parliament building while police fired tear gas and swung truncheons to quell a demonstration outside. Both highlighted the domestic challenges Ahmadinejad faces in attempting to consolidate his power and implement his hard-line agenda.

Ahmadinejad told lawmakers and dignitaries he would dedicate himself to serving the Iranian people and to taking bold steps on the world stage.

"It is not important who voted for whom. What we need is national greatness," he said in a speech broadcast live on television after he was sworn in by the judiciary chief, Ayatollah Mahmoud Hashemi Shahroudi. "We are representing a great nation. It needs great decisions and great deeds. We need to take great steps."

But Ahmadinejad might find achieving greatness a long, hard road, analysts said. He has built his political base on populist economic giveaways and a defiant foreign policy that has won him the fealty of Iran's supreme leader, Ayatollah Ali Khamenei, but which may be difficult to maintain. His unyielding drive may have endeared him to some, but has also led to significant clashes within his own hard-line camp, some members, of which, skipped the ceremony.

"He is facing problems and disputes even among his own … faction, let alone a widening gap with the people outside the government," said Ahmad Shirzad, a political analyst and physicist. "Ahmadinejad started his second term in abnormal conditions, and his popularity is low and weak."

The Obama administration has said it would recognize Ahmadinejad as Iran's leader, though Secretary of State Hillary Rodham Clinton praised the opposition Wednesday during an appearance in Africa.

The governments of the United States, Britain, France, and Germany have said they would not send him a customary note of congratulations, and Ahmadinejad responded with characteristic defiance.

"No one in Iran is waiting for your congratulations," he said. "We do not value your congratulations, and we don't value your smiles."

Despite such bluster, Ahmadinejad faces an emboldened, savvy opposition camp unlike anything Iran has experienced in recent years. The unpredictable and loosely organized protest movement continues to defy authorities and the traditional blunt instruments of state.

Amateur video taken during the inauguration ceremony showed thousands of people gathering around the parliament before they were forcefully dispersed by as many as 6,000 security personnel.

Presidential candidate Mir-Hossein Mousavi and other reformist politicians, emerging as leaders of the movement, continue to publicly question the election results and the government's legitimacy.

"Neither Mousavi nor I have stood back," Mehdi Karroubi, a former parliamentary speaker and also a presidential candidate who boycotted the inauguration, said in comments quoted by several Persian language news Web sites. "We will continue our protests. We will never work with this government. We won't damage the government, but we will criticize its actions."

Ahmadinejad also faces challenges from his conservative rivals, including Parliamentary Speaker Ali Larijani, who presided over Wednesday's ceremony, as well as Tehran Mayor Mohammed Bagher Qalibaf and former Revolutionary Guard Chief Mohsen Rezai, who both skipped it.

Even amid weeks of unrest, fellow conservatives in parliament and elsewhere criticized Ahmadinejad's policies and actions, especially his appointment of a controversial aide, Esfandiar Rahim Mashaei. The president's next challenge will be forming a cabinet, which he must do within 2 weeks.

"He has to give in to the lawmakers and get their consensus," said Sadegh Zibakalam, a Tehran University political scientist. "If he doesn't want to take that course and be stubborn the way he has always been, I believe he will have a great deal of problems with parliament."

Ahmadinejad began his first term as oil prices rose and produced a record windfall, much of which he lavished on popular rural reconstruction projects and low-interest loans. But depressed oil and commodity prices heighten his challenges. Experts predict increased unemployment and decreased investments because of continued insecurity and instability.

The government is bracing for more unrest over plans to cut subsidies and implement a 7 percent sales tax. A Western initiative to sanction foreign companies that sell refined petroleum products to Iran also could strangle the economy.

A unified nation would be better able to weather such a storm, but the Islamic Republic finds itself deeply divided.

"If the government wants to reduce subsidies and make changes to the economy, all walks of society should help and widespread popular participation is needed," said Jamshid Edalatiyan, a Tehran-based analyst with a Swiss market data firm. "Otherwise, the government will fail in its economic policies."

SHOWDOWN FOR THE AYATOLLAHS

In an unprecedented letter to the supreme leader, a group of anonymous clerics challenged his authority. The letter asked the Assembly of Experts to examine whether the supreme leader has become incapable of fulfilling his "constitutional duties." The Assembly of Experts is a body of 86 Islamic scholars charged with electing, reviewing, and removing the supreme leader. The current chairman is Akbar Hashemi Rafsanjani, who recently challenged the establishment.

This is a power struggle between the clerical establishment led by Akbar Hashemi Rafsanjani, Mohammad Khatami, Mehdi Karroubi, and many others against the military wing of the establishment which includes: President Ahmadinejad, Supreme Leader Khamenei, Islamic Revolutionary Guards, Basij milita, and the Guardian Council backed by the hard-line Ayatollah Mesbah-Yazdi. Ayatollah Mesbah-Yazdi is President Mahmoud Ahmadinejad's spiritual advisor. He has been called the most powerful of the hard-line clerics in Qom and strongly opposes democratic rule, the moderates, and reformists. He has considerable influence over the Islamic Revolutionary Guards, Basij milita, Guardian Council, and President Mahmoud Ahmadinejad. He supports suicide bombings, execution of the opposition, and is vehemently anti-West.

In 2005, he issued a fatwa urging Iranians to vote for Mahmoud Ahmadinejad. Subsequently, Ayatollah Mesbah-Yazdi declared that "Iran now had its first true Islamic government and there was no need for any more elections, which were incompatible with theocracy." He supports execution of moderates and reformist opposition and has said that "If anyone insults the Islamic sanctity, Islam has permitted for his blood to be spilled, no court needed either." In a lecture that was released in February 15, 2006, Mohsen Ghorourian, who is a well-known student of Ayatollah Mesbah-Yazdi, said that using the atomic bomb has "religious legitimacy." Caught in the middle of this struggle are the Iranian people ("Green Movement"), who want fundamental democratic changes.

AUGUST 17, 2009

Iranian media report that 28 more people have been put on trial for their alleged involvement in the unrest following the June 12 election. Those in court

Sunday are being tried on charges of plotting the overthrow of the regime.

Mousavi has vowed his new party will continue to "defend the rights and votes of citizens that were crushed in the election."

AUGUST 18, 2009

Former President Mohammad Khatami and Mehdi Karroubi joined the leadership of Mir-Hossein Mousavi's new party "Green Path of Hope Association." Alireza Beheshti, a senior aide to Mousavi, said on Tuesday that Khatami and Karroubi would be members of the party's central council, ILNA news agency reported on Tuesday. "The central council of the Green Path of Hope will be a small group of five to six, including Mr. Khatami and Mr. Karroubi," Beheshti said. He added that the party would also include a "counseling board consisting of 30 to 40 members" who are to be chosen over time, as well as "monitoring committees."

During the inauguration of the new judiciary chief, Sadeq Larijani, Mahmoud Ahmadinejad swiped at Rafsanjani, listed as one of the richest men in the world, as he called for prosecution of "the power holders and the wealthy." Rafsanjani spoke against the consequences of "unjust" verdicts in the trials, saying poor treatment of the detainees will cause society to "descend into chaos." The judiciary chief admitted to deficiencies in the judicial system and pledged to prosecute those who "violated people's rights," Press TV reported.

AUGUST 19, 2009

Mehdi Karroubi said he is ready to present evidence to support his controversial claims that postelection detainees were raped in Iranian prisons.

The head of the Islamic Revolutionary Guard Corps says Mir-Hossein Mousavi should be arrested. Brigadier General Yadollah Javani, who represents Supreme Leader Ayatollah Ali Khamenei in the IRGC, claimed that Mousavi's "Green Movement" of supporters who protested against the results of the June presidential election were established to overthrow the supreme leader.

Allegations that election protesters were tortured and raped in detention must be urgently investigated by the Iranian authorities, Amnesty International's secretary general said on Saturday.

AUGUST 20, 2009

Ahmadinejad's cabinet choices were headed for a rough ride. "Those nominated by the president for government posts must have sufficient expertise and experience; otherwise, a great deal of the country's energy would be wasted," state broadcaster IRIB quoted Parliament Speaker Ali Larijani as saying Thursday.

Mass protests are planned at Ahmadinejad's presence at the annual meeting of the General Assembly of the United Nations. The UN meeting is to begin on September 15th, and Mr. Ahmadinejad's arrival and speech will be on the 23rd of September.

AUGUST 21, 2009

The Iranian speaker of parliament said he is ready to study any evidence about sexual harassment of detainees arrested after the elections, responding to Karroubi's request to present evidence that the detainees were raped and tortured.

AUGUST 22, 2009

Head of the Guardian Council Ayatollah Ahmad Jannati told worshippers at Friday prayers in Tehran that those leaders incited postelection "riots" should be arrested. Meanwhile, several hard-line clerics have raised objections to Mahmoud Ahmadinejad's decision to include three women in Iran's new cabinet

AUGUST 23, 2009

Expediency Council Chairman Akbar Hashemi Rafsanjani said today that Iranian officials and citizens must maintain unity so that the country can deal with its internal and external problems, signaling that Rafsanjani had urged everyone to heed the guidelines set by Supreme Leader Ayatollah Khamenei. This statement signals to many Iranians that Rafsanjani continues to manipulate both the opposition and the establishment for self-interest.

CHAPTER 24 ۲۴

THE WORLD TURNS GREEN

T he world beyond Iran has flocked to support the Iranian citizens' ongoing struggle for freedom from tyranny. Throughout 2009, there has been an exponential amount of new coverage and social networking coverage as well. Most recently, socially and politically conscious celebrities have made their stand to support Iran's "Green Movement."

U2 Supports Iran

U2 is one of the largest, most recognizable names in music today. The group has been established for over 29 years and is still one of the most popular and praised rock bands of all time. The ever so politically active Bono (the band's lyricist) has always taken on the current world events and with the album, *War*, so has U2. Therefore, it is no surprise that during their U2 360 tour, a worldwide extravaganza, the band explicitly set stage time away to devote a song to the Iranian people.

The song, "Sunday Bloody Sunday," was personally dedicated to Iran's "Green Movement" throughout the tour thus far. Creating a suspected motivational outpour of support, the band had the Persian poem "Song of the Reed Flute" by Rumi cascade down the stadium's video screens. As the band drummed and sang and played in pure dedication, the crowd took an emotional moment to enjoy the eternal words of the 800-year-old poet. The many touched souls were evident.

Madonna Plays for Iran

Following in her own footsteps, a concerned Madonna played a song called "Where's My Vote?" during her July 18th tour stop. The video of the performance of the song was displayed on three massive video screens and promoted the message of "finding and using your voice." The song included the lyrics, "get up; it's time; you've got to say what's on your mind" and "the time is right now; say what you like."

The video screens were used for more than theatrical display. The images of the world's most renowned leaders were portrayed one after the other, interchanging with the video showing Madonna dancing and singing amidst a crisp white background. Images of leaders included the faces of

Martin Luther King Jr., Gandhi, Mother Theresa, Bill Clinton, and a snippet of video featuring our most recent leader, President Barak Obama. The features weren't all of famed leaders and influential faces. Video snippets of the people of Iran as they protested and held up their fingers in the form of peace signs adorned the video as well.

Italy Supports Iran

It has been reported that Italy has continued its visual, verbal, and ongoing support for Iran's "Green Movement." Demonstrating their support first was Florence, Italy, or so it is reported. The statement was made that, "Florence was Italy's first city to publicly support Iranian's 'Green Movement,' and is continuing its support by hanging a green banner from the famous Palazzo Vecchio and handing out green wristbands to the audience at Maggio Fiorentino's concert in Boboli Gardens."

Michelangelo's statue of *David* was illuminated with a green light; the statue of *David* is Florence's symbol of opposition against tyranny by an Iranian blogger on BlogSpot this past Wednesday, July 29, 2009. Italy has long been a supporter of Iran, and the country's support continues to be apparent.

Students in Hungary Support Iran

Those who were in Hungary during the past few weeks could get quite confused because their citizens showed a number of different ways of using rallies as a tool of democracy.

On June 19, about a hundred Iranian students studying in Hungary held a silent commemoration at the Heroes' Square in Budapest, the Hungarian capital. The rally had been organized via Facebook. The second demonstration by Hungarian supporters took place in front of the Iranian Embassy in Budapest on June 21. It was called the Green Flashmob.

The Hungarian media reported on the meeting between State Secretary of Foreign Affairs Gábor Iklódy and the Iranian ambassador Ali Reza Irvas, after which the Hungarian official declared that the Iranian protestors had the right to protest peacefully, and that Hungary was concerned about the restraints placed on the media in Iran.

July 25th, United 4 Iran Global Day of Action

United 4 Iran is described as an independent joint venture of individual people and human-rights organizations who promote the restoration of Iran's human rights. The group organized an international rally in support of Iran's "Green Movement" stretching along six countries and 110 cities, including Los Angeles, Brussels, Budapest, Cairo, and Dubai. A unique and diversely ethnic group of society came together, which proved that different beliefs or backgrounds don't equal war!

The United4Iran group says that their goals for the worldwide rally is for civil and human rights for Iran, to work toward an end to the abuse of power, to show proof that the situation in Iran has been noted, and that there is support beyond their pain and struggle.

Breaking news from "citizen journalists," coupled with the news from professional journalists (illegally reporting inside the borders of Iran) has caught the attention of the international media outlets. In reaction to the scenario, the Islamic Republic attempted to prevent the spread of information, and the Clerical Regime has verbally lashed out against foreign countries with accusations of "meddling." According to an article posted on the BBC Web site, the supreme leader has accused, via state TV, the "West," in general, for instigating unrest among the citizens of Iran (which Obama condemns as "unjust" violence). This accusation was continuously plastered all over Iran's state TV in hopes to convince the people that the West was simply constructing the idea of a fraudulent election and feeding it to the Iranian citizens.

The two countries that Khamenei spoke directly about were the United States and Britain. Before the accusations were publically released by the supreme leader, Barack Obama, president of the United States, felt he needed to speak out on the crimes committed by the Islamic Republic. He made this statement which was heard around the world to the Iranian government:

> Mr. Obama said: *"The United States and the international community have been appalled and outraged by the threats, beatings, and imprisonments of the last few days.*
>
> *"I strongly condemn these unjust actions, and I join with the American people in mourning each and every innocent life that is lost."*
>
> He continued: *"The United States respects the sovereignty of the Islamic Republic of Iran, and is not at all interfering in Iran's affairs. But we must also bear witness to the courage and dignity of the Iranian people, and to a remarkable opening within Iranian society."*

These are the comments that invited the accusations of the Islamic Republic and, in their eyes, diminished the credibility of Iran on the international playing field. To say the least, the Islamic Republic was insistent on firing back.

When time came for Obama to answer the accusations of the Clerical Regime, he said:

> *"This tired strategy of using old tensions to scapegoat other countries won't work anymore in Iran.*
>
> *"This is not about the United States and the West. This is about the people of Iran, and the future that they—and only they—will choose."*

At this time when the political dissent had reached its highest levels of violence in Tehran, the Iranian government had already begun to expel, arrest, detain, and even murder, foreign reporters and diplomats. Reporters Without Borders released a statement on June 20th that states, "The Islamic Republic of Iran now ranks alongside China as the world's biggest prison for journalists." The article goes on to say, "The force of the demonstrations in Tehran is increasing fears that more Iranian journalists could be arrested and more foreign journalists could be expelled. The regime has been visibly shaken by its own population and does not want to let this perception endure. That is why the media have become a priority target."

At the same time Khamenei accused the West of meddling, the Islamic Republic demanded that two diplomats from the United Kingdom leave the country immediately. This was obviously no surprise to anyone because of the long history of the negative relationship Iran has had with the United Kingdom, especially Britain.

Mr. Brown, the prime minister of the United Kingdom, told the BBC:

> *"We want a very good relationship with the Iranians; we also respect the fact that it's for the Iranian people themselves to choose who their government is.*
>
> *"But when there is a sign of repression or where there is violence that's affecting ordinary people in the streets, we have a duty to speak out and to say we want Iran to be part of the world, we don't want Iran to be isolated from the world."*

An analyst of the BBC offers this suggestion as an explanation of the relationship between Iran and Britain: "There is a deep-rooted belief in Iran that Britain is always up to something, is never passive, and is always devious. I meet it all the time with Iranians. It is a combination of history and current British involvement with Iran. One issue is the setting up of the BBC Persian TV channel. Another is the presence in the UK of the Iranian opposition group MKO."

THE MOVEMENT'S PLACE IN HISTORY

The common phrase "History repeats itself ..." has seemed to be one of the worst enemies of the Iranian people. Political analysts, both native and foreign to Iran, have always doubted the success of any civilian uprising against the Islamic Republic. Since the fall of the Shah in 1979, there has been an uprising initiated by the student population about every 3 to 4 years. Obviously, all were unsuccessful. So the question is if the "Green Movement" has any chance at success, what factors that weren't present in any other uprisings will contribute to it?

Reza Aslan, for *The Daily Beast,* interviewed Batebi, who had this to say on the differences between the movements:

"The biggest difference between 1999 and 2009 is that the people are wiser and far more experienced at dealing with the regime. In 1999, we were hot and angry and unfocused. The protesters of today are much more calm and purposeful, more experienced. They know how to deal with the government."

It has clearly been with the recent orders given by the supreme leader in regards to the ban on and manipulation of almost all forms of communication in Iran that technology has been recognized as a threat to the Clerical Regime. (The word "technology" here refers to mobile telephones, computers, and the Internet.)

The phrase, "manipulation of the media" generally implies that media, in whatever form (print, electronic, etc.), can be controlled in a manner and for a purpose that is at odds with the original intent of the venue. This claim is subject to circumspection by advocates of either side when presented on a level playing field. However, the true nature of this manipulation is often clouded with rhetoric from the various factions participating in the alleged manipulation. In the case of Iran's complaint that the call by President Ahmadinejad for Israel to be "wiped off the map" was a media exaggeration bears evidence to the fact that some words, even if excised from the original corpus, do not lose any significant meaning.

While it is true than an inflammatory vocabulary can encourage a perceptual distortion of the facts, it is the context that provides the interpretive weight for most readers. Suppression of media is also a form of manipulation. Virtually every country in the world participates in this form of manipulation.

Some, such as Iran, appear to exercise a much heavier hand if measured against the set of observable occurrences. Conventional coverage and associated manipulations focus upon the relationships and simple dichotomies between two opposing concepts or forces. It avoids context that might minimize the intended impact. The more subtle form of manipulation examines issues that are economic, historical, cultural, or political. These elements are clearly absent from most state-run content.

As it relates to the "Green Movement" of 2009, manipulation via suppression of media came in various forms starting with the limiting of cell phone services and the disabling of text messaging. This served to constrain the ability to evaluate content put forth by the state-run radio and television venues. Internet filtering only added to the blatant expression of manipulation by the state-run media outlets and inflamed both the local and international community's sensibilities in this respect.

It would be easy to say that the 1999 student uprisings also used technology, but it is important to recognize the technological advancements that have taken place over the last decade. Advances in tools and techniques related to the creation of software development, coupled with the capitalistic market-driven availability of inexpensive powerful computers and related hardware provided a growing user population with the capability to realize a close-coupling of world events. Much of the hardware infrastructure necessary for the social media network did not exist or was mostly unavailable in 1999.

However, certain breakthroughs in super-cooled microwave receivers, such as used in cell phone transmissions, enabled the rapid deployment of fixed point-of-presence wireless high-speed Internet technology. This technology quickly became a viable alternative to copper and fiber optic lines. The tethered Internet user was a thing of the past. Shortly thereafter, the rate of growth of Internet users began to double nearly every month. In 2003, MySpace™ was launched and "instant messaging" (SMS) became a staple of cell phone users, especially the young, urban, and mobile. In 2005, YouTube was launched and quickly became an overwhelming success, and by 2006, there were an estimated 92 million Web sites online.

The press, which has been restricted by the Islamic Republic, has been forced to confidentially circulate the events of the movement and the ideas of the people active in the movement. Support for Mousavi, including his political platform, have been undeniably flooding international news and the newest form of press, the social media networks. In addition, as the news spreads, the world has become more aware that this movement is not necessarily about Mousavi, but about the Iranian people's demand for a new democratic regime.

After the student attacks that ignited the 1999 student uprising, the supreme leader knew in order for the Clerical Regime to justify the actions of its Basij militia, it must manipulate the public's perspective on the recent events. With that being said, Khamenei pulled a stunt in convincing Khatami to switch roles with him in regards to their responses on the attacks on state TV. The news showed Khatami, the reformist president praised by the student population, threatening the students with harsh consequences if the acts of government dissent did not cease. On the same news footage, Khamenei, the hard-line supreme leader that ordered the closing of the *Salam* newspaper, was showing sympathy for the injured students.

Across the television, footage of pro-government counterdemonstrations were continuously played for the public to watch, exaggerating the number of people that were actually in support of the Clerical Regime. In an article published in *The New York Times* on July 18, 1999, Elaine Sciolino writes, "Unlike the unpredictability and chaos of the student protests, this performance was planned and scripted and the players knew just what their roles were."

All scenes from the previous days of the student uprising were turned around in a way that showed the Islamic Republic as the victim of dissent by the students for no apparent reason. Sciolino continues in the article with, "It was left to the reformist newspapers to publish both sides of the story and print the rest of the images, including photos of students bloodied by vigilantes and female protestors crammed into cages mounted on police cars."

THE TECHNOLOGICAL REVOLUTION

Many international critics have questioned the commonality of digital devices owned among average Iranian citizens. The fact of the matter is, in the city of Tehran, which has a population of 7,800,000, there are 5,500,000 cell phone users. Seeing that the student population is coming from everywhere but mostly the university setting, it is likely that these students make up the large majority of cell phone users in Tehran and throughout Iran.

"[The chairman of the Telecommunications Company of Iran's board of directors] said that the provinces of Tehran (5.5 million), Isfahan (1.4 million), Fars (1.2 million), Hamedan (1.18 million), and Khuzestan (1.12 million) rank first to fifth respectively in terms of the number of cell phone users. Underlining that the cell phone network would witness the highest growth in the year to March 2008, he predicted that given the planning in the sector, five million new SIM cards would be offered to applicants, putting the total number of cell phone users at 28.5 million."

With this many cell phone users in a country, it would seem logical for the country to be filled with a variety of cell phone handsets made by different manufacturers, just as one sees in any other country. Although this statement is valid in regards to Iran, there is one mobile phone company that Iranian citizens don't support, and that they actually boycott—Nokia. This opposition against Nokia Siemens Network was sparked when news that the company was "selling communications monitoring systems to Iran" hit the streets (Saeed Dehghan).

A particular Iranian journalist, jailed from information collected by this "communications monitoring service," said, "And the most unbelievable thing for me is that Nokia sold this system to our government. It would be a reasonable excuse for Nokia if they had sold the monitoring technology to a democratic country for controlling child abuse or other uses, but selling it to the Iranian government with a very clear background of human rights violence and suppression of dissent, it's just inexcusable for me. I'd like to tell Nokia that I'm tortured because they had sold this damn technology to our government."

The rejection of Nokia products by Iranian citizens has greatly affected Nokia's demand in Iran. A Nokia wholesaler in Iran stated, "… I can say that there is half the demand for Nokia's product these days in comparison with just one month ago, and it's really unprecedented. People feel ashamed of having Nokia cell phones." Iranians are sickened by the betrayal of this company, when, in fact, they are one of the leading providers of cell phone products to the Iranian people. The people know that Nokia offers better functioning phones and phones that get the best service in Iran, but despite this, they still refuse to support this two-faced company.

Now common in Iran, accompanying the increase in mobile cell phones, is the high-speed Internet access that users can connect to with always-on instant access. By 2007, more than 1.1 billion people were interacting with the Internet. A glut of third-generation cell phones with built-in high resolution cameras and video recorders ushered in 2008, and the economic downturn of 2009 served only to lower their price and increase availability. The stage is now set with new props that are readily pressed into service and adapted for the pursuit of human endeavor.

It is obvious that with digital media tools like mobile phone and high-speed access to the Internet, there are various avenues that news can be released to the mainstream media outlets, even with the Islamic Republic's tight restrictions on Iran's press and media. Rebecca Santana, reporting for The Associated Press, states, "The Internet has been a key tool for Iran's opposition on two fronts. One is internal—to organize protests and exchange information. The other is external—to let the world know what is going on amid severe government restrictions that bar foreign media from reporting and taking pictures and videos on the streets. The government has been actively trying to block activists on both fronts."

"In spite of government efforts to manipulate public perceptions, Iranians quickly took to the Internet as protests over the election results mounted," James Jay Carafano stated in his article "All a Twitter: How Social Networking Shaped Iran's Election Protests."[1] The Internet, used as a way to inform the world of the events happening within Iran, has been an ever-growing trend among Iranian citizens.

An article written by The Associated Press states, "Around a quarter of Iran's 65 million people are believed to have Internet access. Iran has long used filtering to restrict certain news and political or pornographic Web sites. But since the election, the number of blocked sites have increased." I would offer that "the number of blocked sites has increased" is a *severe* understatement. Research was recently released by Arbor Networks, an Internet security company, that shows Internet traffic on June 13th, 2009, the day that followed the presidential election, almost came to a standstill within Iran due to government control. Although Internet access has become slightly more available to Iranian citizens, social media sites, news media sites (especially the BBC), sites in support of the opposition, and Mousavi are still being blocked.

Many have asked how Iranian people can be "tweeting," posting video to YouTube and updating their Facebook status when they are, in fact, claiming that the government has stopped all Internet access. The answer is simple. These Internet users have found ways to bypass the censored sites, and at the same time have been able to keep their Internet activity undetected by officials. Here are some of the ways that the Iranian people are able to access the Internet:

The most popular method for bypassing censorship is through the use of proxy servers, servers that sit between the point of origin and ultimate destination, which is often enough a service that has been blocked by the government. The user connects to the proxy service and is rerouted and disguised.

Some users, particularly those worried about government repercussions, seek more sophisticated methods of protection. If you find any activist living in the country of Iran, they will further confirm that they "care very much that no one can figure out where your IP address is," said Andrew Lewman, executive director of the Dedham, Mass.-based nonprofit group, Tor Project Inc.

Tor is one of a number of groups that have devised methods for circumventing government censorship. It has software and services that link users to volunteer node providers that route traffic through three separate networks in hopes of defeating traffic analysis, which used to try to deduce who you are dealing with from the source and destination of IP traffic. Its services are agnostic: it can be used by police, bad guys, journalists, and activists—anyone.

Twitter

Some technologies are more amenable to revolution than others. In the case of Twitter, the ability to digitally broadcast to a vast audience of "followers" on multiple devices from cell phones to computers to PDAs is key. The constraint of 140 characters is, in this case, a blessing because it forces a concise representation that demands focus upon the subject in order to communicate a complete, if not succinct, thought. The brevity and breadth of the medium serve to focus the message and its impact on the target audience.

Twitter has enabled both citizens and journalists to inform the international audience of events happening within the borders of Iran despite the even more harsh press restrictions the Clerical Regime has implemented. With heightened consequences for journalists publishing news in support of dissidents, Iranians have, instead, been able to use Twitter to release texts, videos, and pictures from the front lines of the battles occurring within the country. (As has become established custom on Twitter, users have agreed to mark, or "tag," each of their tweets with the same bit of type—#IranElection—so that users can find them more easily.)

Social media analytic company Sysomos has done some great analysis on Twitter users in Iran. According to Sysomos, the number of Twitter users in the country increased from 8,654 in mid-May to 19,235 in mid-June, after #iranelection. Between June 11 and June 19, the nature of tweets from these users changed. On June 11, Iran Twitter users were writing about "Mousavi," "freedom," and "vote." On June 19, they were writing about "Mousavi," "Tehran," and "protest." Also, the percentage of #iranelection tweets coming out of Iran changed from 51.3 percent on June 11 to 23.8 percent on June 19, as a result of the international interest in the postelection protests.

One Iranian citizen, now famous among the international media as "persiankiwi" on Twitter, reported on events as they unfolded on the front lines in Tehran. CNN, the major news corporation, even began to post "persiankiwi" tweets on their site. This unknown person has been the most talked about reporter covering the presidential campaign, election, and aftermath. This story, alone, goes to show the influential role that technology has played in the transformation of journalism in regards to the "Green Movement."

This unknown person who only used the identity, "persiankiwi," was constantly and consistently "tweeting" from before the fraudulent election until 2 weeks after the election had occurred. The following are the last known messages that were sent on June 25, 2009, by "persiankiwi" before she was reportedly detained by authorities:

- they catch ppl with mobile—so many killed today—so many injured—Allah Akbar—they take one of us

- they pull away the dead into trucks—like factory—no human can do this—we beg Allah for save us—

- Everybody is under arrest & cant move— Mousavi—Karroubi even rumor Khatami is in house guard we must go—don't know when we can get internet—they take 1 of us, they will torture and get names—now we must move fast—

- thank you ppls 4 supporting Sea of Green—pls remember always our martyrs—Allah Akbar— Allah Akbar—Allah Akbar

- Allah—you are the creator of all and all must return to you—Allah Akbar—

Just as Twitter can rally protesters against governments, its broadcast ability can rally them quickly and efficiently against news outlets. One such spontaneous protest was given the tag #CNNfail, using Internet slang to call out CNN last weekend for failing to have comprehensive coverage of the Iranian protests. This was quickly converted to an e-mail writing campaign. CNN was forced to defend its coverage in print and online.

Many have called the increasing use of Twitter within the Iranian "Green Movement" the "Twitter Revolution" of Iran, as if the social networking network has already saved—or is going to—the citizens of Iran from their hard-line government. Many analysts and critics have denounced the idea of the "Twitter Revolution" because of its exaggeration of Twitter's capabilities. Twitter, as its own entity, does not possess the ability to rescue a population from their corrupt government. On the other hand, Twitter has been recognized as an effective tool in the "Green Movement" by allowing the world to see, hear, and read about the events occurring on the front lines of the struggle for human rights.

To better understand the difference between "Twitter as a tool" and Iran's "Twitter Revolution," we will refer to Mark Hannah's, writer for MediaShift, article, "How Will Iranian Protests Change Twitter?" He suggests, "Twitter and YouTube may have become powerful expressions told for existing sentiment, but acknowledge that they don't, by themselves, create that sentiment. What will be most interesting," he suggests, "is how Twitter will be used moving forward."

The role of Twitter in these Iranian elections and resulting protests has been immeasurable in the sense of "citizen journalism." Countries found Twitter so useful in delivering news from the source of the protests that many feared the announcement made by Twitter that it needed to shut down for routine maintenance. CNN was the first to report that the United States State Department had urged Twitter to delay its maintenance due to the critical events that were occurring in Iran. The United States did not want to cut off their only source of news from within the country for an unnecessary period of routine maintenance. Their request was acknowledged, and the Twitter network never went down.

Facebook

Facebook provides yet another venue for multimedia expression that is amplified in its expressive power by an inherent simplicity of operation. The suspension of this service by the Iranian government during the June 12th election served only to strengthen claims of the "Green Movement" protesters and the world at large regarding manipulation of the media via suppression of the social media network press.

Facebook seemed to not only be used as an activism tool after the allegedly fraudulent election in Iran, but also as a campaign tool for Mousavi as he rallied support for his party. Before the election, it is said that just one of the Facebook pages in support of Mousavi had already attracted more than 5,200 followers, or "friends," as they call it, on Facebook. There were no such pages showing support to Mousavi's main opponent, the current Iranian president, Ahmadinejad. On May 23, 2009, a little more than 2 weeks before the election was to be held, the Facebook Web site had been blocked to all Iranians in the country. Regardless of who requested or implemented the block on the site, it was still another display of the Islamic Republic violating the rights of its citizens.

It didn't take long for the media or the Facebook company to get wind of this news, and both reacted with outrage. "We are disappointed to learn of reports that users in Iran may not have access to Facebook," the company told AFP in a statement. The company went on to say, "It is always a shame when countries' cultural and political concerns lead to limits being placed on the opportunity for sharing that the Internet provides."

YouTube

"YouTube is the biggest video news site on the Internet, and at no time in our site's history was that more apparent than in these last two weeks of the crisis unfolding in Iran," said Olivia Ma, a member of YouTube's News and Politics team, in a post on the official Google blog.

Perhaps the most compelling and visceral form of social media technology is the video. "Green Movement"-related cell phone images and videos uploaded via the Internet to YouTube have numbered in the thousands and confirm in every imaginable way the impact of street-level citizen reporters upon the views and impressions of events playing out upon the world stage. With over 3,900 postings to date, the quantity alone provides yet another poignant statistic of the human desire for expressive freedom in the fight for democracy, human rights, and human dignity.

YouTube has also been blocked by the government in Iran. Just as all the other social media sites, Iranian citizens are still able to access YouTube and upload their mobile phone videos by using things like proxy servers and Tor. Web traffic from the country to YouTube has dropped by about 90 percent, according to Beet.tv. This single statistic shows just how powerful this media tool has been in enlightening the world on the happenings within Iran's borders.

Although YouTube rose to prominence as a place where users could upload clips of their cats or post videos of skateboarding tricks, the site is becoming an increasingly important tool for the citizen journalism movement.

A YouTube video capturing the death of the young woman named Neda Agha-Soltan instantly elevated her to an icon. Her name, Neda, became the symbol of the new so-called Green Revolution against the theocracy that has endured for 30 years in Iran. Instantly transmitted imagery and tweets about an icon whose death took place only minutes before has perhaps defined this as a cyberwar, and the world was with the passionate young revolutionaries.

The raw footage of Neda's death and hours of protest can be easily found on YouTube, but I was particularly struck by the content of two video compilations, shown below, both of which speak of the social consequences of world events tied together by social media and citizen journalism.

A young American says before he saw the clip of Neda, he didn't really care what was happening in Iran because it didn't affect him. And yet, he was transformed by viewing the video of Neda's death. He says he came to understand that instead of what to him had been just a movie, "these are normal, average human beings … no different" from him except "they don't speak the same language. Those people in Iran," he exclaims, "are fighting for their actual freedom, and they're willing to die for it." His commentary is remarkable considering his self-described apathy toward the entire culture was reversed in a heartbeat by viewing one shocking clip.

The new site offers short instructional videos. They were produced by organizations such as *The New York Times, Washington Post*, and NPR and are designed to teach average citizens the skills to better report on events happening around them in areas sometimes off limits to or out of reach of mainstream news outlets.

After many foreign journalists from mainstream media outlets were barricaded in their hotels or forced to leave Iran in the wake of disputed elections earlier this month, many protesters turned to sites such as YouTube and Twitter as a way of broadcasting video and news to the outside world and giving the international community a firsthand look at the uprising.

Dangers for People Using These "Tools"

The advancement of technology and programs have undoubtedly changed the dynamics of the "Green Movement" in comparison to Iranian uprisings in the past. It would be ideal to say that all of this momentum, moving the country in the right direction, comes at no cost—but that simply isn't a reality for the Iranian people. Unfortunately, the use of things like social media networks, blogs, and e-mail to leak information from Iran is a crime in the eyes of the Islamic Republic that is deserving of some of the harshest punishments.

Along with the popular tools mentioned previously, blogging has also become extremely popular among the student population of Iran. The trend of blogging among students actually became popular far before the 2009 presidential elections. As the violent events have transpired in Iran in regards to the fraudulent election, blogging has become extremely more dangerous now than ever before.

ReadWriteWeb, an organization in support of the safety of Iranian bloggers, posted a news release in regards to blogging in Iran on July 4, 2009:

"The Iranian Parliament is set to debate a draft bill that would add a number of crimes to the list of those that can result in execution, among them establishing weblogs and sites promoting corruption, prostitution, and apostasy."

According to the Islamic Republic, they are heightening the consequences for these types of crimes in order to benefit the civilians of Iran. They see the elimination of weblogs as a way to "strengthen mental security," as if weblogs themselves have the power to control the human mind.

The Committee to Protect Journalists (CPJ) has recently published a list of the "10 Worst Countries to be a Blogger In." Not at all surprising, the CPJ ranks Iran number two on their list with this explanation:

> Authorities regularly detain or harass bloggers who write critically about religious or political figures, the Islamic revolution, and its symbols. The government requires all bloggers to register their Web sites with the Ministry

of Art and Culture. Government officials claim to have blocked millions of Web sites, according to news reports. A newly created special prosecutor's office specializes in Internet issues and works directly with intelligence services. Pending legislation would make the creation of blogs promoting "corruption, prostitution, and apostasy" punishable by death.

After more than a month of detention, several journalists may face trial on charges of "sending pictures to enemy media." Three documentary filmmakers were arrested at the end of July and that brought the total of journalists held in Iranian jails to 42, the highest count in the world.

The journalists are expected to be among 20 unnamed defendants tried on an array of charges, according to a government statement posted by the semiofficial *Fars News* agency. All were arrested in the aftermath of the disputed June 12 presidential elections.

The official Iranian News Agency (IRNA) reported on Wednesday that photographers Majid Saeedi and Satyar Emami confessed to taking pictures and sending them to "enemy [news] agencies." Few details are available about Emami, who was arrested on July 9. Security forces arrested Saeedi, a photographer for several local newspapers and the global photo agency Getty Images, on July 10. Getty has more than 300 photographers working around the world and has offices in Gaza, Islamabad, London, Tokyo, and Iraq, among other countries.

"Majid Saeedi is a well-regarded photojournalist who was simply recording the reality he observed and distributing his photos through a global news agency recognized for its nonpartisan coverage of world events," said CPJ Executive Director Joel Simon. "We are gravely concerned that Saeedi, Satyar Emami, and the many other journalists in jail could be put on trial merely for doing their jobs."

On June 30, *Fars News* agency posted an 11-page "confession" from detained *Newsweek* reporter Maziar Bahari, in which he allegedly said he participated in "promoting a color revolution." Bahari was arrested on June 21 in Tehran. More than 100 journalists representing 47 countries have sent a petition to the Iranian authorities calling for Bahari's release.

In another development, police arrested at least three documentary filmmakers today when thousands of people gathered at Behesht-e-Zahra cemetery to commemorate the killing of Neda Agha-

Soltan, a protester shot in the aftermath of the disputed June 12 election, according to international news reports. Police detained filmmakers Jafar Panahi, Mahnaz Mohammadi, and Rookhsare Ghaem Ghami, according to multiple sources. The BBC Persian service reported that police also arrested Panahi's wife and child, whose age was not mentioned.

Near the end of July, Korosh Javan, a freelance photographer, was released, CPJ has learned. Javan was arrested on July 9. Authorities released on bail Shadi Sadr, a journalist, lawyer, and activist, who was arrested on July 17. Sadr is an editor for the *Women in Iran*, the Web site for a local women's rights group.

Iran has confirmed that it is holding 150 people arrested after the election, according to the U.K.'s *Guardian* newspaper. Other sources cite higher numbers. At least 36 journalists arrested since the crackdown are currently in jail. An additional six journalists were already imprisoned prior to the elections.

Not only has this influx of the use of social media networks fueled the growing flames of the "Green Movement," but it has also changed the face of modern journalism. The recent reelection of

Iranian President Mahmoud Ahmadinejad has resulted in mass protests throughout Iran. Many Iranian protesters believe that the elections were rigged and that their reform candidate, Mir-Hossein Mousavi, didn't get a fair play. Much of the news out of Iran has been focused on the clashes between police and protestors.

Although the Iranian regime has banned foreign coverage of these protests, Iranian citizens have quickly filled the void by providing some dramatic images of these protests. I commend the Iranian people's determination to tell their stories through the news media. Iranians are blogging, tweeting, and uploading videos of these protests. These citizen semijournalists are serving as part advocate for their cause and part journalist to tell a wider public about their story. This may be the future of journalism as we know it.

Pro-Government Supporters Jump on Technology Bandwagon

After witnessing the effective use of digital media tools to enlighten the world on the tragic events occurring in Iran, the Islamic Republic has decided that they, too, need to join the online battle against the opposition.

Although there has been an increase in pro-government activity in the areas of digital media and social networks, this is not seen as anything surprising or alarming by both Iranian people and the international audience. It seems that the Clerical Regime is trying to suppress the digital efforts of the opposition on the Internet just as they are attempting to suppress the opposition's activity on the streets.

This is not the first time that the Islamic Republic has established a presence on the Internet. President Mahmoud Ahmadinejad has had his own blogs, in English and Persian, and the Revolutionary Guard put out a call online for 10,000 bloggers to spread its views.

WHERE THE MOVEMENT IS HEADED

 National revolutions can be traced back hundreds of years. Iran is a country that has been plagued with revolutions, attempted revolutions, and years upon years of political dissent displayed by its citizens. There is no doubt that this country has been suffering political unrest for the last 150 years. Due in large part to its structure of government, Iran's citizens have been obviously robbed of their basic human rights in the shadows of an illusory "democracy." Iran is far from the democratic façade it puts up on the international stage. The fact is that this shadow of powers, cast by the supreme leader and his regime, still darkens the country of Iran.

> *"The other surprise for these gentlemen was that they were thinking that after 12 June (the day of the election), people would go back to their homes after a few rallies, but the fact that a nation with such extent and after all these immense sacrifices is still on the street after more than 40 days shows the depth of this movement; but then again, these gentlemen are imagining that these are a couple of groups from outside the country, and by contacting embassies, this issue can be resolved.*

They were thinking that parties are leading this movement, and, therefore, arrested leaders and figures of the parties and did their best to obtain confessions [from them]."

—Mousavi

When asked about what the two opposition leaders will do now, Mr. Karroubi said: *"We will continue to protest. We will never collaborate with this government. We do not want to hurt them, but we will criticize their actions. In no way will we help."* He added that *"We do not consider this a legitimate government."*

As new events are unfolding each day in Iran, the future of Iran and its people is in no way certain. There are many paths which this conclusion can take, which I warned of from the beginning. We could discuss the ideal situation for the Iranian citizens, the reality of the people if the government is successful in stifling their fight, or a combination of both and the implications each will have on the country of Iran. Using my better judgment, I have decided to focus on the third option.

As with every topic, even those not so interesting, intellectuals have their ideas and theories with which they compose and use to flood the endless academic journals.

In his book covering the Iranians' views on social and political issues, Behzad Yaghmaian presents "a very harsh and negative image of the regime, reflecting the assault conducted against the protest of the university students in July of 1999." He addresses the fact that Iran's population will not allow the Islamic Republic to regress back into their ways of governing before the election of Mohammad Khatami in 1997. The only option, Yaghmaian suggests, is to continue the progression, regardless of the time it takes, towards a democratic government that separates church and state. He goes on to suggest that the idea of a complete separation of church and state within Iran is a naïve and overly optimistic goal. This is unrealistic because of Iran's historical Islamic foundation.

Yaghmaian doesn't leave us hanging on to a severe problem without a solution. He suggests that the solution to Iran's ongoing political unrest and the increasing violations against the Iranian people can be found by looking at the history of other countries that are also strongly rooted in Islamic fundamentals. Other countries that have faced similar situations as Iran, concerned with merging Islam and government, are Iraq and Afghanistan. Iran needs to look at Iraq and their "marriage" of Islam and democracy, although Iraq has not completely conquered this situation either.

In conclusion of his take on the solution for Iran's future in terms of the separation of church and state, Yaghmaian claims:

"After the reforms begun under Khatami, this process is in its very early stages. This is the task of both academic intellectuals and religious scholars, and is, of course, a matter of a serious discourse and dialogue. The process is likely to accelerate as a new generation of bright, young, university-educated clerics emerges in Iran, and could constitute a challenge to the conservative and traditional approach and is likely to contribute to the development of the third way. It is likely to provide support for a pluralist Islam, one which will be more compatible with the modern world and postmodern epistemology."[2]

Yaghmaian's book, *Social Change in Iran: An Eyewitness Account of Dissent, Defiance, and New Movements for Rights*, was published in 2002. With the publication date taken into consideration, he wrote this book at a time when Khatami was president, reform changes were being seen within the government, and the citizens of Iran saw the slightest glimmer of hope for their future. Above, he suggested that the process toward a new government will be led by another generation when a generation "of bright, young, university-educated clerics emerges in Iran."[2]

Will the passionate Iranian students desperate for change in this generation be the ones that further this progression in the "Green Movement"? This question, one that is impossible to answer at this point, only further suggests that the political participation seen in the "Green Movement" possesses the potential for change in Iran.

A BBC News expert contributes this prediction for Iran's future: "It is difficult to predict what is going to happen."

Neither the government nor the opposition are necessarily in a winning position, and among parliamentarians and the Assembly of Experts there appear to be differences in opinion on how to best to move forward.

President Ahmadinejad's government will have to take into account the wishes of all the Iranian people, and unless rapid and tangible reform is initiated, it would be quite difficult to imagine how the government could prevent demonstrations in the future, even if it succeeds in clamping down on the current demonstrators.

Last week's demonstrations were centered in the center of Tehran, mainly in the area around the University of Tehran and Azadi Square. Demonstrations also took place in a number of other towns, such as Shiraz, Esfahan, Tabriz, and Yazd, but many other major towns, such as Mashhad, have been relatively quiet.

However, unless the opposition manages to spread the demonstrations to other parts of Tehran and other cities around the country, or nationwide strikes are organized, for example, by oil workers and the *bazari* (merchant class), it would be difficult to imagine that the demonstrators could continue their protests indefinitely."[4]

The demonstrations mark the largest uprising in the capital Tehran since the revolution days in 1978 and 1979. The world holds its breath while brave Iranians continue to defy the serious violence and murder of government militias. And now, the regime is trying to gag the international press. We can only hope that this does not mean that the authorities are planning even more drastic measures to stop the demonstrations.

Supreme leader Ali Khamenei has asked the Guardian Council to carry out an assessment of the election. This may mean that the Iranian leaders take the situation seriously. Regardless of the choice of president, Ali Khamenei is the one who has all political power, and the Guardian Council must approve all important decisions in parliament. The current situation in Iran marks a shift in the Iranian revolution. There have been deep political and ideological differences in Iran over many years, but the current demonstrations are different from earlier protests. Until now, protests against the regime lacked real broad political unity and support, and have not mobilized large crowds in Tehran.

CONCLUSION

THE WORLD AWAITS A DEMOCRATIC IRAN

The Iranian people have shown the world that they demand open elections, political reforms, and respect for human rights. In addition, the vast majority of Iranians would like to get the country out of isolation, both diplomatically and economically. Iranians are educated, progressive, and largely pro-American. Iran's enormous potential as a cultural and political superpower remains unexpressed if its highly educated population cannot participate in an open and democratic society.

The following days in Iran will be crucial in determining the future of the country. Regardless of what happens further, the international community must continue their support for democratization. At the same time, the rest of the world must help to open communication lines with the Iranian people and distance themselves from the Clerical Regime. This applies especially to the United States. Obama must show clear judgment by distancing his administration from open-ended or backdoor talks with the current regime. With Mahmoud Ahmadinejad as winner of the presidential election, direct dialogue with the Iranian "people" instead of the regime will be even more difficult than we hoped, but all the more necessary. Hopefully, the world will pursue the correct path as the Iranian people lead the nation towards freedom, democracy, and prosperity.

NOTES:

1. James Jay Carafano, "All a Twitter: How Social Networking Shaped Iran's Election Protests," *Right Side News* (July 21, 2009) at <http://www.rightsidenews.com/20090 7215605/editorial/all-a-twitter-how-social-networking-shaped-irans-election-protests.html>.

2. Behzad Yaghmaian, *Social Change in Iran: An Eyewitness Account of Dissent, Defiance, and New Movements for Rights,* (2002).

3. Christopher Rhoads and Geoffrey A. Fowler, "Iran Pro-Regime Voices Multiply Online" at <http://online.wsj.com/article/SB124658 422588090107.html> (July 3, 2009).

4. Viewpoints: "What's Next for Iran?" at <http://news.bbc.co.uk/2/hi/middle_east /8112829.stm#sadjadpo> (June 23, 2009).